NURSING
PROFESSIONALS

PRACTICAL CAREER GUIDES

Series Editor: Kezia Endsley

Computer Game Development & Animation, by Tracy Brown Hamilton
Craft Artists, by Marcia Santore
Culinary Arts, by Tracy Brown Hamilton
Dental Assistants and Hygienists, by Kezia Endsley
Education Professionals, by Kezia Endsley
Fine Artists, by Marcia Santore
First Responders, by Kezia Endsley
Health and Fitness Professionals, by Kezia Endsley
Information Technology (IT) Professionals, by Erik Dafforn
Medical Office Professionals, by Marcia Santore
Nursing Professionals, by Kezia Endsley
Skilled Trade Professionals, by Corbin Collins

NURSING PROFESSIONALS

A Practical Career Guide

KEZIA ENDSLEY

ROWMAN & LITTLEFIELD
Lanham • Boulder • New York • London

Published by Rowman & Littlefield
An imprint of The Rowman & Littlefield Publishing Group, Inc.
4501 Forbes Boulevard, Suite 200, Lanham, Maryland 20706
www.rowman.com

6 Tinworth Street, London, SE11 5AL, United Kingdom

British Library Cataloguing in Publication Information Available

Library of Congress Cataloging-in-Publication Data

Names: Endsley, Kezia, 1968– author.
Title: Nursing professionals : a practical career guide / Kezia Endsley.
Description: Lanham : Rowman & Littlefield Publishing Group, [2020] |
  Series: Practical career guides | Includes bibliographical references. |
  Summary: "Nursing Professionals, which includes interviews with professionals in the field, covers the following areas of this field that have proven to be stable, lucrative, and growing professions. RNs, LPNs, Nurse Practitioners, Nursing Assistants, Orderlies"—Provided by publisher.
Identifiers: LCCN 2019042555 (print) | LCCN 2019042556 (ebook) | ISBN 9781538133118 (paperback) | ISBN 9781538133125 (epub)
Subjects: LCSH: Nursing. | Nursing—Vocational guidance.
Classification: LCC RT42 .E53 2020 (print) | LCC RT42 (ebook) | DDC 610.73—dc23
LC record available at https://lccn.loc.gov/2019042555
LC ebook record available at https://lccn.loc.gov/2019042556

♾️™ The paper used in this publication meets the minimum requirements of American National Standard for Information Sciences—Permanence of Paper for Printed Library Materials, ANSI/NISO Z39.48-1992.

Contents

Introduction

A career in nursing can be a long, varied, and rewarding journey. © *FatCamera/E+/Getty Images*

Welcome to a Career in Nursing!

If you are interested in a career as a nurse, you've come to the right book. The nursing field is a varied, flexible, exciting, rewarding, and highly in-demand career. Nurses serve as the glue that holds a patient's healthcare journey together. Their job is both science (making treatment decisions and giving medications) and art (identifying or intuiting a patient's needs and providing care). They provide services pertaining to the diagnosis, evaluation, and prevention of diseases and disorders; well-being and preventative services; disease management; assistance in surgical settings; emergency medical services; and many other forms of aid.

There is a lot of good news about this field, and it's a very smart career choice for anyone with a passion to help people. It's a great career for those who get energy from working with other people and want to help others get and stay healthy. Job demand is high; there continues to be a shortage of nurses entering the workforce compared to the rising need for nurses.

> "Nurses are really valuable in a society! They are often the unsung heroes."
> —Kiann Payne, inpatient nurse case manager

When considering any career, your goal should be to find your specific nexus of interest, passion, and job demand. Yes, it is important to consider job outlook and demand, educational requirements, and other such practical matters, but remember that you'll be spending a large portion of your life in whatever career you choose, so you should also find something that you enjoy doing and are passionate about. Of course, it can make the road easier to walk if you choose something that's in demand and lucrative. That's where the nursing profession really shines!

What Is a Nurse?

A nurse is a professional healthcare provider who gives medical and other attention to those in need. Nurses work in hospitals, medical offices, surgery rooms, schools, clinics, out in the field, and even in war zones. A good nurse cares for *and* advocates for his or her patients. The nurse is often one of the few people on a healthcare team who sees the whole patient in their environment and can advocate for the person rather than simply treat the illness or injury. This requires a good mix of skills, both soft (empathy, intuition, respect for the patient) and hard (critical thinking, time management, scientific and medical knowledge).

Nursing Careers

There are so many different roles for nurses that this book can't possibly cover them all—check out the sidebar to see just some of the many options. In this book, you will meet seven nurses and talk about careers in nursing from many different points of view.

THE MANY FACES OF NURSING

Acute care nurse practitioner

Advanced practice nurse

Ambulatory nurse

Anesthesiology nurse

Bone marrow transplant nurse

Burn unit registered nurse

Cardiovascular nurse

Certified nurse-midwife

Charge nurse

Chief nursing officer

Director of emergency nursing

Director of nursing

Emergency room nurse practitioner

Geriatrics nurse practitioner

Home health nurse

Hospice care nurse

Internal medicine nurse

In-vitro fertility nurse

Labor and delivery nurse

Long-term care nurse

Maternal and child health nurse

Neonatal (NICU) nurse

Nurse anesthesiologist

Nurse manager

Obstetrics nurse

Oncology nurse

Operating room nurse

Pediatric nurse

Surgery nurse

Transplant nurse

Travel nurse

Wound and ostomy care nurse

Types of Nursing

This book covers the four main nursing areas currently active in the United States, based on their roles and responsibilities. These are listed in order of least amount of education needed to most:

- Certified nursing assistants (CNAs)
- Licensed practical nurses (LPNs), called licensed vocational nurses (LVNs) in some parts of the country
- Registered nurses (RNs)
- Advanced practice registered nurses (APRNs)

In addition, chapter 1 touches on a promising profession related to nursing, the physician assistant.

So what exactly do these types of nurses do on the job, day in and day out? What kind of skills and educational background do you need to succeed as a nurse? How much money can you expect to make, and what are the pros and cons of being a nurse? How do you avoid burnout and deal with stress? Is this even the right career path for you? This book can help you answer these questions and more.

"You don't get to be a good nurse overnight—you work at it."—Sandra Gooden, clinical nurse educator and acute care nurse for over forty years

---

This book includes interviews from real professionals working as nurses. The goal is for you to learn enough about nursing in all its variations to give you a clear view as to which aspects, if any, are a good fit for you. If you still have questions, the book ends with a list of resources where you can learn even more.

An important note: If you choose a career within the healthcare umbrella, you need to have a lifelong curiosity and love of learning. Your education won't be over once you finish your degree. In fact, maintaining certifications and meeting or exceeding continuing education requirements (usually set forth by some governing board and/or by state regulations where you practice) are very important in all the healthcare fields, including nursing.

The Market Today

The United States Bureau of Labor Statistics forecasts that the field of nursing in general will grow about 12 percent during the decade of 2018 to 2028,[1] which is much faster than the average profession. (See https://www.bls.gov/emp/ for a full list of employment projections.) Not only does this translate into job security, but it also means that more new positions are being created every year.

> According to the January 2012 "United States Registered Nurse Workforce Report Card and Shortage Forecast" in the *American Journal of Medical Quality*, a shortage of registered nurses is projected to spread across the country between 2009 and 2030. In this state-by-state analysis, the authors forecast the RN shortage to be most intense in the South and the West.[2]

The demand for jobs in nursing continues to grow in the United States due to many factors:

- We have a large elderly population, as the generation of baby boomers continues to age. This population struggles with chronic conditions, such as diabetes and obesity, that require continuous care.[3]
- Growing diseases, disorders, and illnesses, including Alzheimer's disease, cerebral palsy, attention-deficit/hyperactivity disorder, and autism, all demand continuing services from healthcare providers, including nurses.
- Hospitals and healthcare professionals are emphasizing preventive care (often administered by nurses) to help patients recover from cardiovascular and pulmonary diseases and to improve their overall health.[4]

- Treatments in injury prevention and detection continue to evolve and become more complicated.
- Increasing information and expectations from the public about injury treatment and prevention translate to a higher demand for care.
- A decrease in the number of primary care physicians and stricter cost control measures have led to a greater demand for nurses.[5]
- Current nurses are retiring at a rate that's higher than new nurses entering the workforce.[6]

What Does This Book Cover?

The goal of this book is to cover all aspects of your search for a nursing career and explain how this profession works and how you can excel in it. Here's a breakdown of the chapters:

- Chapter 1 explains the four different types of nursing roles in the United States at this time—CNAs, LPNs, RNs, and APRNs. You'll learn what nurses in these roles do in their day-to-day work, the environments in which they work, some pros and cons about each career path, the average salaries of these jobs, and the future outlook for these roles.
- Chapter 2 explains in detail the educational requirements of these different nurses, from doctorate degrees to two-year associate degrees and even certificates. You will learn how to go about getting experience (in the form of shadowing, internships, and fieldwork) in these fields before you enter college as well as during your college years.
- Chapter 3 explains all the aspects of college and postsecondary schooling that you'll want to consider as you move forward. You will learn how to get the best education for the best deal. You will also learn a little about scholarships and financial aid and how the SAT and ACT work.
- Chapter 4 covers all aspects of the interviewing and résumé-writing processes, including writing a stellar résumé and cover letter, interviewing to your best potential, dressing for the part, communicating effectively and efficiently, and more.

Where Do You Start?

Nursing is so vast and varied that you can approach your career from many angles. Are you more interested in the science and biology behind it all, or do you feel that you would be great at working with and helping people? Do you want to work in a high-stress, high-stakes, exciting environment like emergency medicine, or are you more suited for steady work where you build rapport with the same patients over years, such as in an office setting? Do you want to specialize in one area of care, such as labor and delivery or behavioral health, or would you prefer to work as a generalist like a charge nurse, a medical-surgical nurse, or a nurse manager? Are you better with kids and babies, or do you enjoy working with the elderly? The options are nearly endless, and you can change your focus as you age and advance in your career as a nurse.

The good news is that you don't need to know the answers to these questions yet. In order to find your best fit as a nurse, you need to understand how nurses work. That's where you'll start in chapter 1.

Starting your career journey can be daunting, but this book will help! © *sergeichekman/iStock/ Getty Images*

Why Choose a Career in Nursing?

You learned in the introduction that nursing is a large, healthy, and growing career field. You also learned a little bit about how it's split into different roles, depending on your degree and level of schooling. You also were reminded that it's important to pursue a career that you enjoy, are good at, and are passionate about. You will spend a lot of your life working; it makes sense to find something you enjoy doing. Of course, you want to make money and support yourself while doing it. If you love the idea of helping people for a living, you've come to the right book.

As a reminder, this book covers these main areas of nursing: certified nursing assistants (CNAs), licensed practical nurses (LPNs), registered nurses (RNs), and advanced practice registered nurses (APRNs). It also touches on the related role of the physician assistant (PA).

This chapter breaks out these areas of nursing and covers the basics of each. The nice thing is that no matter what degree of postsecondary education you can or want to pursue, there is a way for you to choose a nursing role and be a part of the nursing profession. After reading this chapter, you should have a good understanding of each role and can then start to determine whether one of them is a good fit for you. Let's start with certified nursing assistants.

The Certified Nursing Assistant

The primary responsibilities of a certified nursing assistant revolve around helping patients with their daily activities, such as bathing, dressing, and eating.[1] CNAs work in state, local, and private hospitals and are in high demand in nursing homes and long-term care facilities.

CNAs also serve as intermediaries between the nurses, doctors, and patients. They may be responsible for recording and communicating a patient's issues to the medical staff. Depending on the kind of setting they work in, other duties might include setting up equipment for the nurse or doctor and transporting patients to treatment units and operating rooms. As a CNA, you have to be prepared to work nonstandard hours, including nights, weekends, and holidays.

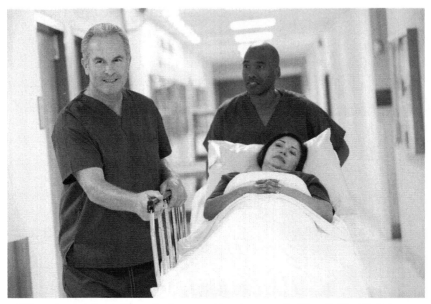

CNAs are in great demand in nursing homes and long-term care facilities. © *iStock/Getty Images*

Training to be a CNA involves learning the basic nursing principles and working hands-on in supervised clinical settings. You can get CNA training at vocational colleges, community colleges, and technical schools, as well as at a few hospitals and nursing homes.

After you've completed the CNA program, you have to take an exam to prove your competency. Only after you have successfully passed this exam are you listed in the state registry as a certified nursing assistant. Different states have different criteria that you will need to meet before you can practice there. Check out your state's board of nursing site to find out what exactly is needed to become a certified nursing assistant in your particular state.

Individuals who are still pursuing higher training often use the CNA position as a way to gain relevant experience. As a student, you can pursue your degree while working as a CNA in a medical facility.

MAIN RESPONSIBILITIES

CNAs:

- Bathe and dress patients
- Take vital signs
- Collect information about conditions and treatment plans from caregivers, nurses, and doctors
- Answer patient calls
- Examine patients for bruises and other injuries/wounds
- Turn or reposition patients who are bedridden
- Lift patients into beds and wheelchairs and onto exam tables
- Clean and sanitize patient areas
- Provide and empty bedpans
- Change sheets and restock rooms with supplies

HOW HEALTHY IS THE CNA JOB MARKET?

The Bureau of Labor Statistics (BLS, www.bls.gov) is part of the US Department of Labor. It tracks statistical information about thousands of careers in the United States. According to the bureau, employment for CNAs is expected to grow 9 percent over 2018 to 2028, which is faster than the national average. CNAs will continue to be in demand as the population ages and more people require extended healthcare treatments or spend time in residential and long-term care facilities.

These statistics show how this career fares now and in the foreseeable future:

- *Education*: Postsecondary nondegree certificate
- *2018 median pay:* $28,530
- *Job outlook 2018–2028:* 9 percent growth
- *Work environment:* In 2018, most CNAs worked in skilled nursing facilities (38 percent) or in a hospital setting (27 percent). A smaller group

worked in continuing care retirement communities and assisted living facilities for the elderly (11 percent).[2]

The Licensed Practical Nurse

Licensed practical nurses, known in Texas and California as licensed vocational nurses, support the healthcare team and work under the supervision of an RN, APRN, or MD. By providing routine care, they ensure the health and welfare of their patients during the healthcare journey. Although LPNs cannot diagnose or treat patients, interpret medical data, or make medical decisions about the patient, the care they provide is vital to the overall well-being of their patients.

To become an LPN, you can pursue an associate's degree in nursing (ADN—usually two years) or an LPN diploma/certificate, which is specialized to nursing topics and usually takes one year. At minimum, LPNs must complete one year of academic training through a diploma or certificate program. Every state sanctions the National Council Licensure Examination for practical nursing (NCLEX-PN), and prospective LPNs must obtain their employer state's support.

Most LPN diploma/certificate programs require twelve months of intensive classroom and clinical work. Students usually complete forty to sixty credits of coursework, which cover fundamental concepts in practical nursing, family nursing, and mental health, before they create and present a final capstone project.[3] All practical nurses must also partake in clinical simulations and training, and online LPN programs include an in-person portion.

MAIN RESPONSIBILITIES

LPNs:

- Check vital signs and look for indications that health is deteriorating or improving
- Perform basic nursing functions such as changing bandages and wound dressings
- Talk to patients and note their responses
- Ensure patients are comfortable, well-fed, and hydrated
- May administer medications in some settings[4]

HOW HEALTHY IS THE LPN JOB MARKET?

The Bureau of Labor Statistics reports that employment for LPNs is expected to grow 11 percent from 2018 to 2028, which is faster than the national average. LPNs are expected to be in great demand as the generation of baby boomers continues to age and our population continues to struggle with chronic conditions.

These statistics show just how promising this career is now and in the foreseeable future:

- *Education*: Postsecondary nondegree certificate or associate's degree (ADN)
- *2018 median pay:* $46,240
- *Job outlook 2018–2028:* 11 percent growth
- *Work environment:* In 2018, most LPNs worked in nursing and residential healthcare facilities (38 percent) or in a hospital setting (15 percent). Another group worked in offices or home healthcare services settings (25 percent).[5]

WHO WERE FLORENCE NIGHTINGALE AND CLARA BARTON?

Clara Barton (left) and Florence Nightingale (right).

If you are truly interested in nursing, you should know about these two ground-breaking women who forged a path to modern, professional nursing.

Florence Nightingale, born in 1820, was an English social reformer and is considered the founder of modern nursing. She first served as a manager and trainer of nurses during the Crimean War of the 1850s, during which time her reputation and that of nursing rose to great esteem. She worked tirelessly to professionalize the role of nursing, including establishing a nursing school in London that still exists today.

Clara Barton, born in 1821 in Massachusetts, was a nurse during the American Civil War and later founded the American Red Cross. During the Civil War, she provided crucial, personal help to soldiers, many of whom were wounded, hungry, and without supplies other than what they carried on their backs. She was not formally trained as a nurse, as there wasn't much formal training at that time; she learned her medical skills and bedside manner from experience and on-the-job training. She was known as the "Florence Nightingale of America."

The Registered Nurse

RNs provide and coordinate patient care in all kinds of settings, wherever care is needed.
© asiseeit/E+/Getty Images

Registered nurses are essentially the backbone of the healthcare system in the United States. They outnumber LPNs in the workforce three to one.[6] RNs provide important healthcare services to the public in various settings. Among other duties, they provide and coordinate patient care, educate patients and the public about various health conditions, and provide advice and emotional support to patients and their family members.[7]

"I want to encourage other guys to enter the nursing field. There is still a very low percentage of men in nursing. This has been a good career for a me as a man in terms of being able to support my family. You can support your family, male or female."—Marc Gavilanez, OR circulator nurse

Registered nurses work in hospitals, doctors' offices, home healthcare settings, and nursing care facilities. RNs also work in outpatient clinics and schools, or serve in the military. Registered nurses usually take one of three education paths—they pursue a bachelor of science degree in nursing (BSN), get an associate's degree in nursing (ADN), or receive a diploma from an approved nursing program. All of these programs require hours of supervised clinical experience in addition to traditional classroom work. Although only an associate's degree is required, having a BSN can help your chances of advancement and better pay. And some employers—especially those in hospitals—require a bachelor's degree. Other employers may hire you with an ADN but require you to earn your BSN within a few years of employment.

A research survey by the American Association of Colleges of Nursing (AACN) shows that nurses with BSNs have better patient outcomes, including lower patient mortality rates, than their ADN counterparts. The research also indicates that BSN holders have higher proficiency in making good diagnoses.[8] In 2010 the Institute of Medicine called for increasing the number of BSN-prepared nurses in the workforce to 80 percent by 2020.[9]

Registered nurses must also be licensed. To become licensed in the United States and Canada, you must pass the National Council Licensure Examination for registered nurses (NCLEX-RN).10 Chapter 2 covers these educational and professional certification requirements in more detail.

MAIN RESPONSIBILITIES

RNs:

- Perform physical exams and health histories before making decisions
- Provide health promotion, counseling, and education
- Administer medications and other interventions
- Organize and provide care, in collaboration with a wide array of healthcare professionals[11]

AN OB NURSE'S PERSPECTIVE

Stacey Hummel.
Courtesy of Stacey Hummel

Stacey Hummel received her bachelor's degree in nursing in 1999 from the University of Indianapolis and then earned her master's degree in nursing administration and leadership at Ball State in 2016. She has worked as an obstetrics (OB) nurse her entire career, twenty years at a small county hospital. She has been managing the OB/maternity nurse department since 2015.

How did you become interested in nursing?

My grandmother was a maternity nurse at the pediatrics office where I went as a kid. She always had great stories about how she was helping people and she worked with children and infants. She was smart, well-spoken, and respected. She was my role model! I wanted a career that challenged me academically, but helping people also appealed to me. I liked biology, anatomy, and physiology and wanted to do something challenging. I originally thought about becoming a physical therapist, so I shadowed that job in high school and found that I did not like it. Shadowing is really a great opportunity to see what you actually like.

What are the main job duties of an OB nurse?

An OB nurse has two patients—the mom and the baby (either newborn or unborn). You have to master the basic nursing concepts, of course, but especially concepts in women's healthcare. Neonatal healthcare too. We are with the mothers during the labor and delivery process. Emergent situations come up. You have to be sharp and quick on your feet. You have to recognize subtle changes and be in tune with your patient. Postpartum care involves tons of education—you teach the mothers how to care for their infants. It has a very heavy patient education focus. Most of your patients are fairly healthy and young. After the critical labor and delivery, it's all about educating the mothers. Your goal is to make them feel confident and empowered to take care of their infant!

As an OB nurse, you do see and treat preterm labor, high blood pressure, and chronic illnesses on top of [the women] being pregnant. You get really close to your patients in a short amount of time. I find it very rewarding and satisfying. It's a "happier" area than some others in nursing, as most of the patients are fairly healthy.

I am now managing the OB nurse department. I love leadership. Being a charge nurse was the first step, and I did that for fifteen years. As a manager, I deal with staffing and scheduling, and I work with the managers to help develop the culture of the unit. When the manager position came open, I was ready and I wanted to lead and make policies and decisions.

I help "grow" the nurses now and help them with their careers and with education. However, I also maintain all my skills. We are in office more as managers, but I am still out there enough to keep my skills sharp.

In nursing, there is a lot of advancement and opportunity for growth over the course of a career.

OB is intense and it can wear on your nerves after a while. So I don't mind being a little farther removed from the day-to-day after so many years. It's a physically taxing job and that's hard as you get older. It's smart to plan for the next step and be practical about career moves. However, as a manager, you should never ask someone to do something that you can't do yourself!

How did your education prepare you for your job?

First off, I really appreciated my science courses in high school—biology, anatomy, and physiology. I had to take them again in college, but having that background really helped cement those concepts.

Nursing school is very intense, just like the job. The University of Indianapolis gave me a great education and I was well-prepared. It was one year of general classes and three years of clinical experience, plus nursing-specific classes and complementary classes. There is a lot of on-the-job learning also. The skills are simulated in nursing school (on manikins, etc.), but until you are at the bedside and work with actual people, you can't be 100 percent prepared. Some stuff you just have to learn to on the job.

Multitasking and other soft skills to be a professional are things you learn on the job. Think about finding a mentor on the job that can teach you [technical] skills but also help with professional skills—timeliness, multitasking, having a routine, etc.

I did a whole semester on OB/pediatrics. It's not always done that way. You go through all the different clinical areas. Med-surg (basic) is highly emphasized, then build off that for other specialties—ER, surgery, pediatrics, psychology.

What's the best part of being a nurse?

Seeing a family be healthy and leave with a healthy newborn is very fulfilling. And they pay you to do that! That never gets old. You are helping people become parents! It's an honor and a privilege. You get to be part of their intimate moments.

As a manager, I love to see new nurses get more confident, grow their skills, and learn more. They learn to see the big picture too.

It's also a very flexible job. There are so many different areas to work in, and it's great for family life (because of the flexible hours). You are well compensated also.

What is the most surprising thing about OB nursing?

Once you know everything that could go wrong, it's so amazing that so many moms and babies come out healthy and normal. It's the norm that things will be okay. It's a miracle!

However, one surprising thing is the high maternal mortality and infant mortality in the US—it's the most dangerous place to have a baby in the developed world! This is a focus of mine, to make this better.

It's also sad and surprising to see the number of "broken" people we get—drug-addicted people, homeless people, and patients with mental health issues. You must have a "service heart" and try to help them no matter what. It's hard to feel like you always make a difference in these cases.

What are some challenges facing the nursing industry at this time?

The nursing shortage is a real problem. Nursing has done itself a disservice by having the different levels of preparation for the same job (ASN and BSN). They often do the same work and get paid the same. So many people get the ASN, but the BSN-prepared nurse is safer according to research, and that's what hospitals want. However, there is a shortage and they want people out of school faster. But that's not safer. We are trying to make a standard. Studies show that having 80 percent of BSN-prepared nurses is the best case. (At my hospital, we hire ASNs and then require that they get their BSN within three years. We also have tuition reimbursement and scholarships.)

Health crises such as opiates, maternal mortality, etc., are also issues, but we can solve these with effort. Substance abuse by nurses is high, maybe as high as 20 percent. The stress and trauma is very hard to deal with, and that can lead to substance abuse. We need to debrief those situations and talk about them. Supporting and caring for yourself is very important for your mental and physical health. The profession needs to do a better job caring for nurses too.

What are some characteristics of a good nurse?

You need to be a strong student. You should also be a people person in most areas: be comfortable chatting with people and getting to know people, be a good communicator, and think outside the box when teaching or communicating with patients. You'll meet patients with different languages, from different cultures, and you have to find ways to connect with them. You need to be flexible, compassionate, and caring.

I look for people who are leaders and are professional.

What advice do you have for young people considering a career in nursing? How can a high schooler prepare for a career in nursing?

Take your schooling seriously. Study the sciences, but don't limit yourself to them. Learn how to write and speak well.

Job shadow in high school in an area of nursing where you have interest. Talk to a current college student in a nursing program. Know what it is before you commit to the program and the profession.

While in nursing school, get a CNA job or a patient care tech job. School is so much easier when you already have exposure to the actual job. You can be a CNA in high school even. Get your hands on it as soon as you can. It exposes you to all the issues around dealing with patients.

HOW HEALTHY IS THE RN JOB MARKET?

For anyone studying to become an RN, the news is great! Employment is expected to grow 12 percent from 2018 to 2028, which is much faster than the national average for other professions. RNs are expected to be in great demand as the generation of baby boomers continues to age and our population continues to struggle with health issues.

These statistics show just how promising this career is now and in the foreseeable future:

- *Education*: Usually a bachelor's degree (BSN), although an associate's degree (ADN) is acceptable in many places. All states require RNs to be licensed.
- *2018 median pay:* $71,730
- *Job outlook 2018–2028:* 12 percent growth
- *Work environment:* In 2018, most RNs worked in hospitals (60 percent) or for ambulatory healthcare services (18 percent). A smaller group worked in nursing and residential care settings (7 percent).[12]

The jury is in: registered nurses enjoy a promising and lucrative career!

> "Nursing is a great career. The flexibility is great—there are so many different areas of nursing and there is something for everybody. If you don't like your current job, you can try another area or specialty."—Sarah Sprunger, cardiac progressive care nurse

The Advanced Practice Registered Nurse

Advance Practice Registered Nurses usually have at least a master of science in nursing (MSN), in addition to the standard nursing education and licensing required for all RNs. A doctor of nursing practice (DNP) is quickly becoming the preferred level of preparation in this field. APRNs serve four specialized and specific roles in the healthcare field—nurse practitioners, certified nurse-midwives, clinical nurse specialists, and certified registered nurse anesthetists.

APRNs provide crucial primary and preventative healthcare to the public. For example, they treat and diagnose illnesses, advise the public on health issues, and manage chronic disease states. They are often considered just one step under the doctor. As an APRN, you should be prepared to engage in continuous education to remain at the very forefront of any technological, methodological, or other developments in the field.

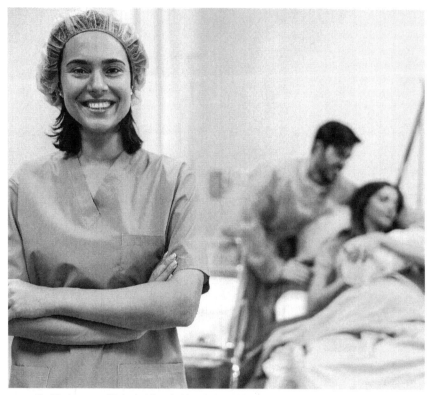

Certified nurse-midwives deliver babies and provide medical care to pregnant mothers.
© pixelfit/E+/Getty Images

APRN ROLES[13]

APRN Role	Description
Nurse Practitioners (NPs)	Prescribe medication, diagnose and treat minor illnesses and injuries, assess patients, order and interpret diagnostic and laboratory tests, and develop treatment plans. They often specialize by patient population, such as the elderly.
Certified Nurse-Midwives (CNMs)	Deliver babies and provide gynecological and low-risk obstetrical care. Provide wellness care to women, which may include family planning, gynecological checkups, and prenatal care.
Clinical Nurse Specialists (CNSs)	Handle a range of physical and mental health problems. They have the skills and expertise to identify where the gaps are in healthcare. They can help design and implement interventions and assess and evaluate those to improve overall healthcare.[14]
Certified Registered Nurse Anesthetists (CRNAs)	Work with surgeons, anesthesiologists, dentists, podiatrists, and other professionals to ensure the safe administration of anesthesia. In fact, they administer more than 65 percent of all anesthetics in the United States.[15]

HOW HEALTHY IS THE APRN JOB MARKET?

The Bureau of Labor Statistics reports that employment for the APRN roles is expected to grow 26 percent over 2018 to 2028, which is much faster than the national average. This explosive growth is due mainly to the increased emphasis on preventive care, as well as the demand for healthcare services from the aging baby boomer population.

These statistics show just how promising this career path is now and in the foreseeable future:

- *Education*: Master's degree (MSN) or doctorate (DNP)
- *2018 median pay:* $113,930
- *Job outlook 2018–2028:* 26 percent growth

- *Work environment:* In 2018, most APRNs worked in an office setting (47 percent) or in a hospital setting (27 percent). A smaller group worked at outpatient care centers (9 percent).[16]

Of the approximately 240,000 APRN jobs in the United States in 2016, 116,000 were held by nurse practitioners, 42,000 by nurse anesthetists, 72,000 by clinical nurse specialists, and 6,500 by nurse midwives.[17]

The Physician Assistant: A Nursing-Related Role That's Exploding

Physician assistants are licensed to diagnose and treat illness and disease and to prescribe medication to patients.[18] They work in physician offices, hospitals, and clinics in collaboration with a licensed physician. In fact, the physician assistant role falls somewhere between a nurse and a doctor. PAs complete programs that are more in line with the medical model. That means that while nurses follow a patient-centered model, physician assistants follow the disease-centered model of doctors.

The physician-PA relationship is very important to the profession and can greatly enhance the quality of the healthcare that patients receive. Because of their advanced education in general medicine, physician assistants have a lot of autonomy in treating patients.

To become a physician assistant, you must earn a bachelor's degree first, which takes roughly four years. Undergraduate students often pursue a major in the field of science, but the major itself is less important than taking the right prerequisites, which may include:

- Anatomy and physiology
- Biology
- Chemistry
- Mathematics or statistics
- Microbiology medical terminology
- Healthcare ethics[19]

Qualifications vary from state to state, but most physician assistants become licensed after completing a four-year degree followed by a twenty-five-month accredited physician assistant program and then a one-year clinical rotation.

MAIN RESPONSIBILITIES

PAs:

- Take medical histories
- Perform physical exams
- Order and interpret laboratory tests
- Diagnose and treat illnesses
- Educate and counsel patients
- Assist in surgery
- Prescribe medicine
- Assess and record a patient's progress[20]

HOW HEALTHY IS THE PA JOB MARKET?

These statistics show just how promising this career path is now and in the foreseeable future:

- *Education:* Master's degree
- *2018 median pay:* $108,610
- *Job outlook 2018–2028:* 31 percent growth
- *Work environment:* In 2018, most PAs worked in an office setting (55 percent) or in a hospital setting (26 percent). A smaller group worked at outpatient care centers (8 percent).[21]

PAs have a growing role in providing healthcare services because they can be trained more quickly than physicians. Team-based healthcare models will continue to evolve and become more commonly used. Physician assistants are an important part of that team-based model. They can expect to participate in all areas of medicine as states expand allowable procedures and autonomy, and as insurance companies expand their coverage of physician assistant services.[22]

Which Type of Nursing Is Best?

Now that you've read about the various roles nurses can take and degrees they can earn, you are probably wondering which one is best for your circumstances. That's going to be an individual decision based on several factors, including your ability and desire for long-term schooling and the kind of nursing you want to practice. The following table summarizes the characteristics of the four main roles so you can get a good idea of which best fits your career needs and personal goals.

If you want to be involved in treating patients and making decisions about their healthcare regimen, then CNA or even LPN might not be the best fit. The bottom line: the more responsibility and autonomy you want, and the higher the salary you expect, the longer you'll have to stay in school. Many prospective nurses begin schooling in CNA or LPN programs, which are shorter and less expensive. Once the nurses are licensed, they work in those fields while pursuing their BSN or MSN. Using that approach, you can test the professional waters, make a living, and advance your career as you work toward a higher-level nursing degree. In those cases, you may also find that your employer provides tuition reimbursement to help pay for your BSN degree.

	Degree Needed (Years in School)	Average Annual Salary	Advancement Opportunities	Main Work Setting
CNA	Certificate (less than 1 year)	$28,000	Not readily available	Long-term care facilities
LPN	Certificate (1 year) or ADN (2 years)	$45,000	Better if you have an associate's degree	Long-term care facilities
RN	ADN (2 years) or BSN (4 years)	$70,000	Need BSN for increased autonomy, supervisory roles	Hospital settings
APRN	BSN (4 years) and MSN or DNP (2–6 years)	$114,000	First line of healthcare; lead and supervise	Office settings

The Pros and Cons of Being a Nurse

The nursing field is healthy and growing, as you've learned in this chapter. If you choose to become a nurse, you'll enjoy a lucrative salary and real job security. In addition to security, the nursing profession typically affords flexible work hours and allows you to practice part-time without negative ramifications. Because nurses are needed all over the country (and beyond), you will find it much easier to secure a new job after a move than many of your non-nurse friends.

Also, because nursing is practiced in many different settings, the day-to-day environment can vary greatly, which means you can find the kind of workplace that matches your needs and personality without leaving your profession. Maybe the greatest pro associated with this career is that you'll also be able to help people during their time of need.

Despite nursing's many advantages, there are a few cons to consider as well. One rather large hurdle is how rigorous the schooling and licensing process can be. Although some registered nurses do practice with an associate's degree, it's becoming more and more common for employers to require a BSN, especially if you want advancement and new opportunities. That BSN includes lots of math and science. In fact, if you don't enjoy the sciences, you probably shouldn't consider the nursing field.

Another issue to keep in mind is the physicality of the job. You will be on your feet and working hands-on with patients all day. This can lead to chronic physical issues, such as back pain, that you need to be ready to manage and treat.

In addition to physical stress, the mental stress of the nursing profession is well documented. Even though working with others can be a great source of joy and satisfaction, dealing with patients can also be a source of stress. Whether it's patients with a terminal illness, patients who don't comply with their treatment regimen, or overall difficult or noncompliant patients, the burden of caring for human beings can take its toll.

And, as with all healthcare professions, there is always the risk of infection and exposure to viruses and germs when working around patient populations, especially if you work in a hospital, nursing home, or healthcare facility.

Am I Right for the Nursing Profession?

Ask yourself these questions:

- Do I like meeting, talking with, and helping people?
- Am I comfortable around people who are sick or disabled?
- Am I detail-oriented and able to handle multiple tasks at once?
- Am I a critical thinker, and can I act quickly on my feet?
- Am I ready to spend most of my working day on my feet?
- Do I enjoy learning about the biology of the human body?
- Do I mind touching people I don't know or could I learn to be comfortable with this idea?
- Am I ready to be an advocate for my patients?
- Can I handle the emotional issues that accompany dealing with people who have chronic physical or cognitive issues and potentially diminished capabilities?
- Am I ready to give advice that might not be followed, even if it's best for my patients? Can I accept that not everyone will do what's best for themselves?

If the answer to any of these questions is an adamant no, you might want to consider a different career path. However, keep in mind that many of these skills can be learned and honed if you have the right attitude and a passion for nursing.

Nursing involves collaborative and cooperative work with the whole
medical team. © *iStock/Getty Images*

A NURSE WITH A PASSION FOR CHILDREN

Kiann Payne.
Courtesy of Kiann Payne

Kiann Payne graduated from Purdue University in 1982 with an associate's degree in nursing and a bachelor's degree in child development/child psychology. She earned her bachelor's in nursing in 1999 from Purdue and then earned a master's in nursing healthcare systems management in 2010.

Her first job was at Riley Hospital for Children in Indianapolis, part of the Indiana University Health network, as a neonatal intensive care unit (NICU) nurse. She then moved to California and worked in a pediatric ER and in a pediatric clinic run by a large healthcare system. She also worked in an urgent care center with an industrial medicine specialty before returning to the NICU environment in different hospitals in a few different parts of the country. She has spent the majority of her career working in the NICU or with children in some capacity. After she attained her master's degree, she became a case manager at Riley Hospital for Children, where she still enjoys working in pediatrics.

How would you describe your current position?

I am an inpatient nurse case manager at the Riley Hospital for Children. That means I develop discharge plans for patients going home. I set up all their posthospital care, such as home nursing needs, walkers and wheelchairs, IVs, respiratory equipment, even rides to and from their appointments, return appointments, and more (most of these patients have chronic conditions). I also deal with insurance companies so that IU Health gets paid appropriately and the patents are in the hospital the "right" amount of days. I give status updates to insurance companies, Medicare, and Medicaid, so that the patients are covered appropriately. The third part of my job, since I work at a teaching institution, is teaching the medical staff about insurance coverage: how to document care properly so things are covered appropriately, the correct verbiage to use, etc.

How did you become interested in nursing?

When I first went to college, I didn't know what I wanted to do. I came to realize that I really liked kids and wanted to work with them. I started taking child development and child psychology classes. As I was deciding on that, someone suggested that I look into nursing, which would be a quicker route to working with children. A friend's mom was a nurse and she suggested I look into being a pediatric nurse.

I then could work as a nurse and maybe later pursue a master's or higher degree if I still wanted to do that, which seemed smart to me at the time. I have basically always worked with kids as a nurse since.

Do you think your education prepared you for your job?

I do think that it did. The way that I pursued my degrees really worked for me. I went back later to get a master's degree in nursing. I evolved, and the work I did or wanted to do evolved too. So when I was ready to get the master's, it prepared me for the next step.

What's the best part of being a nurse?

By far, as a career, it allows you to try and do so many different things. You can completely change the things that you do over time. It's stimulating and valuable to change and continue to grow. For example, you can go from being a bedside nurse to working in a clinic to working in case management over the course of your career. There are so many different things you can do as a nurse. The career doesn't get stagnant.

What is the most surprising thing about nursing that you've found over the years?

People value and respect nurses, but since it's mostly females, it isn't always valued from a business point of view. From what they are paid to the lack of input a bedside nurse sometimes has in an organization—these are undervalued. Nurses don't always have a voice that's equal to their knowledge and expertise, and if that were different, the patient population would benefit.

What are some current things in the nursing profession that are especially challenging?

In general, it's particularly challenging right now to recruit and keep nurses. Women are entering lots of other professions, which is great, but it's more difficult to find and recruit nurses. There are not as many male nurses as there should be.

Of those who are nurses, many move out of the bedside nursing role as soon as they can. As an example, the nurse practitioner license is very popular because you can work in clinics and can be more independent. You can work in private industry and hospitals and prescribe treatment plans and meds. So people aren't staying as bedside nurses. It's good that nurses have more opportunities for career growth, but it's generally a problem for the industry. There are terrible bedside nursing shortages in the industry right now.

What are some characteristics of a good nurse?

A good nurse must have good math and science skills. Over time, you need good attention to detail. You need to see what the patients don't tell you, including through their body language. This can be the most important clue to what they really need.

Wanting to help sick and injured people is important too. Having the heart to talk to people and being present in a difficult moment are really important, especially as a bedside nurse. But you must be technically detailed too.

What is the baby boomer effect on the nursing profession?

They bring lots of challenges to healthcare. For one, as they age, all the baby boomer nurses are retiring. There were/are many baby boomer nurses. This has created a nursing shortage. Also, they [baby boomers in general] are a huge population and are aging and requiring greater healthcare services.

It's a golden opportunity to become a nurse at this time. You graduate and you *will* have a job. You will not have to be unemployed, ever!

What advice do you have for young people considering a career in nursing?

Make sure you want to do it. You give a lot of yourself—long hours, and it's intellectually and emotionally draining. Be committed to it.

If you are a lifelong learner and you crave lots of different settings and variety, it might be the best career for you. Plus, it's in great demand and there isn't an end in sight.

How can a high schooler prepare for a career in nursing?

Do things to see if the environment fits you. Volunteer at a hospital, a nursing home, another healthcare facility, etc. That will give you the flavor of it. All hospitals still have volunteers. It can give you the feeling of what it's like to work as a nurse. You'll see nurses do what nurses do.

Any last thoughts?

Nurses are really valuable in a society! They are often the unsung heroes.

Characteristics of a Great Nurse

Regardless of the source you turn to, you'll find the same basic characteristics used to describe a great nurse. Standouts in the nursing field:

- Have a caring nature
- Are empathetic
- Are detail oriented
- Are organized
- Are adaptable
- Are emotionally stable
- Have physical and mental endurance
- Are quick thinkers (and have great judgment)
- Are hardworking
- Are good communicators
- Enjoy cooperative and collaborative work
- Feel comfortable working with the human body
- Feel comfortable motivating others
- Get energy from being around others[23]

If you pursue a career that fundamentally conflicts with the person you are, you won't be good at it and you won't be happy. Don't make that mistake. Need help in determining your key personality factors? Take a career counseling questionnaire to find out more. Look online or ask you school guidance counselor for reputable sources.

Summary

In this chapter, you learned a lot about the different roles that nurses can take in the healthcare world—CNA, LPN, RN, and APRN. You also learned about the physician assistant role, which is midway between a nurse and a doctor. You learned about what nurses in these roles do in their day-to-day work, the environments where you can find these people working, some pros and cons about each career path, and the average salaries and projected growth of these jobs. You hopefully even contemplated whether your personal likes and preferences meld well with these roles. At this time, you should have a good idea what each role looks like. Are you starting to get excited about one area of nursing over another? If not, that's okay, as there's still time.

An important takeaway from this chapter is that no matter which of these areas of nursing you might pursue, it will be very important to maintain licensure and meet continuing education requirements. Advances in understanding in the fields of medicine, pharmacology, nutrition, and more are continuous, and it's vitally important that you keep apprised of what's happening in your field. You need to have a lifelong love of learning to succeed as a nurse.

> "To be a good nurse, you have to be a lifelong learner. Things change often and you have to keep up."—Marc Gavilanez, OR circulator nurse

Chapter 2 dives into forming a plan for your future, covering everything there is to know about educational requirements, certifications, and internship and clinical requirements. You'll learn about finding summer jobs and making the most of volunteer work as well. The goal is for you to set yourself apart—and above—the rest.

2

Forming a Career Plan

Now that you have some idea which area of nursing you want to find out more about—or maybe you even know which one you will start pursuing—it's time to formulate a career plan. For you organized folks out there, this can be a helpful and energizing process. If you're not a naturally organized person, or if the idea of looking ahead and building a plan to adulthood scares you, you are not alone. That's what this chapter is for.

After discussing ways to develop a career plan (there is more than one way to do this!), the chapter dives into the various educational requirements of the nursing profession. It also looks at how you can gain experience through internships, volunteering, clinic work, shadowing, and more. Yes, experience will look good on your résumé and in some cases it's even required. But even more important, getting out there and experiencing a job in various settings is the best way to determine whether it's really something that you will enjoy. When you find a career that you truly enjoy, it will rarely feel like work at all.

If you still aren't sure which of these nursing roles, if any, is right for you, try a self-assessment questionnaire or a career aptitude test. There are many good ones on the web. As an example, the career-resource website Monster.com includes its favorite free self-assessment tools at www.monster.com/career-advice /article/best-free-career-assessment-tools. The *Princeton Review* also has a very good aptitude test geared toward high schoolers at www.princetonreview.com /quiz/career-quiz.

Your ultimate goal should be to match your personal interests and goals with your preparation plan for college/careers. Practice articulating your plans and goals to others. Once you feel comfortable doing this, you have a good grasp of your goals and the plan to reach them.

Planning the Plan

You are on a fact-finding mission of sorts. A career fact-finding plan, no matter what the field, should include these main steps:

- Take some time to consider and jot down your interests and personality traits. Are you a people person or do you get energy from being alone? Are you creative or analytical? Are you outgoing or shy? Are you organized or creative, or a little of both? Take a career-counseling questionnaire (found online or in your guidance counselor's office) to find out more. Consider whether your personal likes and preferences meld well with the career you are considering.
- Find out as much as you can about the day-to-day aspects of the job. In what kinds of environments is it performed? Who will you work with? How demanding is the job? What are the challenges? Chapter 1 of this book is designed to help you answer these questions for the nursing field.
- Find out about educational and certification requirements. Will you be able to meet any rigorous requirements? This chapter and the next will help you understand the educational paths and licensing requirements for nursing.
- Seek out opportunities to volunteer or shadow professionals doing the job. Use your critical thinking skills to ask questions and consider whether this is the right environment for you. This chapter discusses ways to find internships, summer jobs, and other nursing-related experiences.
- Look into student aid, grants, scholarships, and other ways you can get help to pay for schooling. It's not just about student aid and scholarships, either. Some larger organizations will pay employees to go back to school to get higher degrees.
- Build a timetable for taking required exams such as the SAT and ACT, applying to schools, visiting schools, and making your decision. You should write down all important deadlines and have them at the ready when you need them.
- Continue to look for employment that matters during your college years—internships and work experiences that help you build hands-on experience and knowledge about your intended career.

- Find a mentor who is currently working in your field of interest. This person can be a great source of information, education, and connections. Don't expect a job (at least not at first); just build a relationship with someone who wants to pass along his or her wisdom and experience. Coffee meetings or even e-mails are a great way to start.

A mentor can help you figure out which way to go with your career aspirations.
© LumiNola/E+/Getty Images

"Job shadow in high school in an area of nursing where you have interest. Talk to a current college student in a nursing program. Know what it is before you commit to the program and the profession."
—Stacey Hummel, OB nurse department manager

Where to Go for Help

If you're aren't sure where to start, your local library, school library, and guidance counselor's office are great places to begin. Search your local or school library for resources about finding a career path and finding the right schooling that fits your needs and budget. Make an appointment with or e-mail a counselor to ask about taking career interest questionnaires. With a little prodding, you'll be directed to lots of good information online and elsewhere. You can start your research with these four sites:

- The Bureau of Labor Statistics' Career Outlook site at www.bls.gov /careeroutlook/home.htm doesn't just track job statistics. An entire portion of the site is dedicated to helping young adults uncover their interests and match those interests with jobs currently in the market. Check out the section called "Career Planning for High Schoolers." Information is updated based on career trends and jobs in demand, so you'll get practical information as well.
- The Mapping Your Future site at www.mappingyourfuture.org helps you determine a career path and then helps you map out a plan to reach your goals. It includes tips on preparing for college, paying for college, job hunting, résumé writing, and more.
- The Education Planner site at www.educationplanner.org has separate sections for students, parents, and counselors. It breaks down the task of planning your career goals into simple, easy-to-understand steps. You can find personality assessments, get tips for preparing for school, read Q&As from counselors, download and use a planner worksheet, read about how to finance your education, and more.
- The TeenLife site at www.teenlife.com calls itself "the leading source for college preparation" and includes lots of information about summer programs, gap year programs, community service, and more. TeenLife believes that spending time "in the world," outside of the classroom, can help students do better in school, find a better fit in terms of career, and even interview better with colleges. This site contains lots of links to volunteer and summer programs.

Use these sites as jumping-off points and don't be afraid to reach out to a real person, such as a guidance counselor, if you're feeling overwhelmed.

Making High School Count

If you are interested in nursing, there are some basic yet important things you can do while in high school to position yourself in the most advantageous way. Remember, it's not just about having the best application, but also about figuring out which areas of nursing you actually would enjoy and which ones don't suit you.

- Load up on the sciences, especially biology and anatomy. A head start in anatomy, biology, and/or physiology will be a big help.
- Sign up for psychology. Nurses treat the whole person, not just a body.
- Be comfortable using all kinds of computer software.
- Learn first aid and CPR. You'll need these important skills.
- Hone your communication skills in English, speech, and debate. You'll need them to speak with everyone from doctors to patients in pain.
- Volunteer in as many settings as you can. Read on to learn more about this important aspect of career planning.

> "A good nurse is caring, honest, and empathetic. I always try to remember that each patient is someone's loved one. I try to think how I would want my loved one to be treated."—Deb Newhouse, oncology nurse

Educational Requirements

No matter what degree of postsecondary education you can or want to pursue, there is a role for you in nursing. The following sections cover the educational paths to nursing in more detail.

THE NONDEGREE CERTIFICATE PLAN

To work as a certified nursing assistant (CNA) or a licensed practical nurse (LPN/LVN), you need at minimum a diploma/certificate that's specialized to nursing topics only. This educational process can take from three months to a year, depending on the school and your end goal. Let's break these two roles down further.

Becoming a CNA

Approved CNA diploma programs are typically at least 105 hours; they include at least seventy-five hours of clinical training and thirty hours of classroom education (some states require much more). Each state establishes its own requirements for CNAs and approves the schools/programs that offer certification, so be sure to find a program that's approved by your state. Visit your state's public health department website or www.nursinglicensure.org for more information.

In addition to completing an accredited diploma/certificate, CNAs must become certified by passing an exam. Sixteen US states and the District of Columbia use the National Nurse Aide Assessment Program (NNAAP) for certification purposes. On the NNAAP, candidates must pass knowledge and skills tests. The knowledge test is available in written and oral formats; the oral test includes ten word recognition/reading comprehension questions in addition to sixty oral questions.[1] For more information about the NNAAP, visit www.ncsbn.org/nnaap-exam.htm.

Statistical Data. Recall that the median pay for a CNA in 2018 (the most recent data available at the time of this writing) was $28,530. The job growth/outlook for the decade of 2018–2028 is 9 percent, which is faster than average.

Becoming an LPN/LVN

For LPNs, the minimum is one year of academic training through a diploma or certificate program. That usually includes forty to sixty credits of classroom work, which cover fundamental topics in practical nursing, family nursing, and mental health. It also includes many hours of hands-on clinical work. Each state establishes its own educational requirements for LPNs and approves the schools offering credentials, so be sure to find a program that's approved by your state[2] (or the state you plan on practicing in, if that's different). Good yearlong programs are offered by hospitals, junior colleges, community colleges, and technical schools, so check out the ones in your area. Ensure that they provide practical nursing students with the opportunity for supervised clinical experience.

Visit www.nursinglicensure.org for information about the licensure requirements in your state and a comprehensive list of approved schools. It's a good place to find a school that's accredited and meets your needs. The site includes license requirements and process for all areas of nursing.

Although earning a certificate is often the fastest route into the workforce, credits from these programs cannot be used toward further education. If you think you may want to further your nursing education at any later time, such as eventually becoming a registered nurse, earning an associate's degree is your best option for future career goals.

Recall that potential LPNs must also pass the National Council Licensure Examination (NCLEX-PN) sanctioned in their state. Read the sidebar about this exam for more information.

Statistical Data. Recall that the median pay for an LPN in 2018 (the most recent data available at the time of this writing) was $46,240. The job growth/outlook for the decade of 2018–2028 is 11 percent, which is faster than average.

ASSOCIATE'S DEGREE IN NURSING PLAN

The associate's degree in nursing (ADN) path is required for registered nurses and also may be your best bet as a prospective LPN, especially if you want to further your career at a later time and work toward the registered nurse (RN) role. Earning an ADN is typically a two-year commitment.

An associate's degree in nursing actually refers to a number of different two-year degrees:

- Associate of Nursing (AN)
- Associate Degree in Nursing (ADN)
- Associate of Science in Nursing (ASN)
- Associate of Applied Science in Nursing (AASN)

The differences between these degrees are relatively minor and pertain to additional coursework outside of your core nursing courses. What's important is that all of these degrees provide a quick, inexpensive path to qualifying for the NCLEX exam and entering the nursing workforce.[3]

Keep in mind that community colleges and technical schools can provide a much cheaper way (as little as half the cost) to attain the same degree offered by universities. As long as those programs are accredited, it won't matter to potential employers that you didn't attend a more well-known university.

Getting certified and licensed as a nurse takes hours of clinical work.
© *martinedoucet/E+/Getty Images*

ADN VERSUS BSN: PROS AND CONS

In nursing, an associate's degree (ADN) and a bachelor's degree (BSN) both prepare you to take the NCLEX-RN exam, and you can enter the workforce as soon as you pass the test. But many personal and financial factors may influence your decision of which degree to pursue. Considering these pros and cons of the ADN can help you decide which path is best for you.

Pros to the ADN path:

- It's the entry-level requirement to becoming an RN.
- It allows you to try the field without committing to a four-year program.
- Credits can transfer to a four-year degree if you want to change paths.
- It takes less time so you can enter the workforce sooner.
- It's more affordable.

Cons to the ADN path:

- Your career advancement opportunities are more limited.
- BSN-educated nurses are in higher demand and usually earn a higher wage.
- It doesn't provide the necessary training to pursue a specialty.
- Some employers, such as many hospitals, require a BSN degree. Others may hire you with an ADN but expect you to earn your BSN within a few years of employment.
- The industry is moving toward requiring nurses to have a BSN. If you have an ADN, you may be behind the curve, career-wise.

The BSN is a better option if you are sure you want to be a nurse. If you do decide to pursue an associate's degree in nursing as your entry-level degree, there are many ADN-to-BSN bridge programs that allow you to earn your BSN in a shorter amount of time.[4]

BACHELOR OF SCIENCE IN NURSING DEGREE PLAN

Although registered nurses can and do practice with associate's degrees, it's be-coming more and more common for employers to require a BSN, especially if you want advancement and new opportunities. This hiring trend is a response to an industry-wide push for all nurses to hold baccalaureate degrees. In 2010, the Institute of Medicine (IOM) announced an initiative to create a workforce of 80 percent BSN-prepared nurses by 2020.[5] Perhaps as a result, the bachelor of science degree is now the most popular degree that prospective registered nurses pursue.[6]

The BSN is a higher educational credential than the ADN and usually takes four years to complete. Candidates are eligible to take the NCLEX-RN exam upon receiving their degree, the passing of which is required in order to practice as a nurse. The primary difference between BSN and ADN course content is that nursing theory is explored in greater detail in the bachelor's program.

Having a BSN versus an ADN usually leads to a higher salary, greater responsibility, and a greater chance for promotions in the workplace. (See the sidebar "ADN versus BSN: Pros and Cons," for more comparisons between these two career paths.)

If you are sure you want to become a registered nurse and may eventually want to further your education in the form of a master's (MSN) or doctoral (DNP) degree, the BSN is a better path for you. Here are just a few advantages to the BSN degree path:

- A bachelor's degree enhances career mobility, as most administrative and supervisory positions require a BSN.
- A BSN grants entry to master's or doctoral nursing programs, leading to career advancement and higher salaries.
- The critical thinking skills imparted by a BSN translate to improved patient care and safety.
- Job opportunities outside of traditional floor nursing begin with the bachelor's degree in nursing; these graduates are positioned for a range of specialized nursing jobs.[7]
- Studies show that having BSN-educated nurses results in better medical outcomes for patients.

There are many excellent BSN programs in every state in this country, and many of those can be taken online. Before you enroll in any program, confirm that it is accredited and that all the eligibility and licensing requirements meet your situation. As part of any BSN program (even an online offering), you'll need to complete a clinical rotation prior to graduation.

NURSING AS A SECOND CAREER

Sarah Sprunger.
Courtesy of Sarah Sprunger

Sarah Sprunger has worked as a nurse since 2010. She earned her associate's degree in nursing from Marian University, Indianapolis, having entered nursing school with a bachelor's degree in criminal science/communications. She currently works in a cardiac progressive care unit as well as in an ER department (part-time at both places).

How did you become interested in nursing?

My undergraduate degree was in criminal justice and communications. I had, late in my college career, become interested in nursing and had a friend who was doing nursing. But I felt I was so far along in getting my degree that I didn't want to add on more time and money. I was burned out on school and ready to graduate.

Nursing was always on the back burner for me. I worked as a paralegal for a while, but I never loved it. It wasn't personally fulfilling or enriching. I wanted something that would be more enriching instead of just punching a clock. So, in 2006, I started working on my prerequisites for nursing school. In 2010 I graduated with my ASN.

Do you think your education prepared you for your job?

Yes. The ASN is sufficient for passing the nursing boards. The BSN is a more in-depth program, and it's more well-rounded. Your clinicals give you a little bit of an idea of what you'll be doing.

The hands-on aspect of the schooling/clinicals had diminished right before I attended. This was hospital-driven due to legal concerns. I think this was detrimental; my clinicals weren't as great as I had hoped. There was more watching and less hands-on doing. Nursing is hands-on.

In addition to the classroom and clinical experience, I really learned a lot from my nurse mentors once I had my first job. New nurses at hospitals have an extensive on-boarding/shadowing process (twelve to sixteen weeks), where they are paired with a senior nurse. This mentoring process was really helpful. It was very beneficial to me—I got more out of that than I did out of clinicals.

What's the best part of being a nurse?

You may do something that has a very positive long-term impact on someone's well-being. On the flip side, a bad day can be really, really bad. You're doing a lot of positive things without recognition or pats on the back. Sometimes family members do reach out and it feels great. More practically, the flexible scheduling is very nice, especially when you're a parent or have other obligations. Holidays and weekends can be a drag, but scheduling and hours are so very flexible. The type of nursing you do can vary greatly and also is very flexible—you can do bedside, education, management, work with kids, etc. It never gets old.

What is the most surprising thing about being a nurse?

It's definitely not for someone who is squeamish. It's not an easy job. You'll have your hands doing things and in things you might not expect! The smells can also be hard to take. You don't know how you will handle these types of situations until you're in the thick of it! That's the reason I've seen people change careers or get away from bedside.

I am also surprised by the micromanaging of the nurses that goes on in departments sometimes. The push to computers and electronic medical records is shifting the focus to the screen and away from the patient. Checking the right boxes on-screen can take away from actually caring for the patient. You need to still hear the patient or family and connect with them and not be so involved in the computer.

Critical thinking of nurses is important, and e-charting takes away from that critical thinking. You did what you were supposed to do, but you didn't do right by the patient. Patients even complain about it. They think it's eroding the quality of patient care, and they have a point.

How much hand-holding is involved with patients surprised me too—literally and figuratively. Patients and their families need more of it than I expected. Especially with someone at the end of life—what I realized is you are taking care of the loved one's family too, not just the loved one.

What are some characteristics of a good nurse?

You must have good time-management skills or you will drown. You need to be good at critical thinking. You need to be able to assess and evaluate a situation pretty quickly. Communication is also very important. It's less about being book smart, in my opinion. Awesome nurses don't have to be book smart; they just need to get the bigger picture and think on their feet. You also need to know your limitations and know when to ask for help. Know who your resources are—you are part of a medical team.

What advice do you have for young people considering a career in nursing?

It's a great career. The flexibility is great—there are so many different areas of nursing and there is something for everybody. If you don't like your current job, you can try another area or specialty. There are great opportunities for advanced practice nurses as well. You can take your education as far as you want. It's also a great career for people with families, because of the flexibility.

How can a high schooler prepare for a career in nursing?

One thing I wish I would have done is volunteer at a hospital or at clinics. You can get exposure during high school. You are always a student as a nurse—there is always something to learn. The more exposure you have, the bigger your knowledge base. In school, I could always point out the students who worked in hospitals as students (as techs and aides, CNAs, etc.). They were better prepared in school and as new grads entering the workforce.

Statistical Data for RNs

Recall that the median pay for an RN in 2018 (the most recent data available at the time of this writing) was $71,730. The job growth/outlook for the decade of 2018–2028 is 12 percent, which is faster than average.

WHAT IS THE NATIONAL COUNCIL LICENSURE EXAMINATION?

The National Council Licensure Examination is an examination for nurse licensure in the United States and Canada. Prospective nurses are required to pass the NCLEX in order to be licensed and practice.

There are two types of the exam: the NCLEX-RN (registered nursing) and the NCLEX-PN (practical nursing). After graduation from a school of nursing, the candidate takes the NCLEX exam to receive a nursing license in his or her state of practice.

NCLEX examinations are developed and owned by the National Council of State Boards of Nursing, Inc. (NCSBN). The NCSBN administers these examinations on behalf of its member boards, which consist of the boards of nursing in the fifty states, the District of Columbia, and US territories. See www.ncsbn.org/nclex.htm for more information.[8]

GOING BEYOND: THE MASTER'S AND DOCTORAL DEGREE PATHS

In order to practice as an APRN (advanced practice registered nurse), you'll need a master's of science in nursing (MSN). Recall that individuals licensed as APRNs usually practice in one of these four roles:

- Nurse practitioner (NP)
- Certified nurse-midwife (CNM)
- Clinical nurse specialist (CNS)
- Certified registered nurse anesthetist (CRNA)

The MSN is a graduate degree, so it's a higher educational level than the bachelor of nursing (BSN) but not as advanced as the doctor of nursing practice (DNP). Most MSN programs require that you have a BSN for admission, although there are some RN-to-MSN bridge programs available for qualified candidates. The MSN is one way to distinguish yourself from the many BSN-level nurses working in the field.

The MSN is usually a two- to three-year program that requires students to focus their studies in a certain area. That might be a clinical specialty, such as women's health, anesthesia, or oncology, or a career path, such as nursing administration or nursing education. The MSN is the first step in the credentialing process required for the specialized professional practice positions mentioned above.

Although MSN programs are expensive and financial aid is not common at the graduate level, many employers help pay tuition costs for qualified employees. Very good MSN programs are available online, which makes it easier to earn your degree while working as an RN. In fact, many working nurses complete the MSN in two years without leaving their full-time jobs.[9]

Some benefits of getting your MSN degree include:

- APRNs (i.e., nurses with master's degrees) enjoy the highest salaries in the field of nursing.
- A forecasted shortage of physicians means that advanced practice nurses will continue to assume roles of greater clinical responsibility.
- Nurse educators will also enjoy growth in the job market, as most of today's nursing instructors are expected to retire soon.
- The MSN is a requirement for many careers in nursing, including the most lucrative and in-demand positions, such as the nurse practitioner and the nurse anesthetist.[10]

The MSN also prepares students to earn a doctorate of nursing practice, which is the terminal degree in the field (that means there is no more advanced degree after that).

Most DNP candidates enter the program with an MSN degree, although some programs do allow BSN students. You can expect to complete the DNP

The American Association of Colleges of Nursing (AACN) is now recommending that the DNP be the minimum standard of education for all APRNs. It is not a requirement at this time, but all APRNs specialists (certified nurse-midwives, nurse anesthetists, nurse practitioners, and clinical nurse specialists) will eventually be required to have the DNP, as opposed to the MSN.[11]

in three to six years, depending on the program, your schedule, and your educational starting point. (As you might imagine, BSN students usually take much longer to earn a DNP.) The program's content is focused on statistics and data analysis, leadership skills, advanced clinical skills, and nursing philosophy.[12] The DNP is a practice-focused degree that concentrates on evidence-based improvements. This is in comparison to a PhD in nursing, which is more research-focused and is not covered at length here.

As our healthcare system continues to evolve, DNPs will take on bigger roles in problem solving and advocacy, as well as work in collaboration with other areas of medicine. This increased responsibility comes with higher pay rates and opportunities for advancement, especially as current DNP holders start to retire. You should know that there has been controversy over the DNP degree and how (or if) it is that different from an MSN program or even a PhD. Before you make the significant time and financial commitment to a DNP program, be sure it is the best approach to meet your goals as a nurse.

Statistical Data for APRNs

Recall that the median pay for an APRN in 2018 (the most recent data available at the time of this writing) was $113,930. The job growth/outlook for the decade of 2018–2028 is 26 percent, which is faster than average.

Experience-Related Requirements

You've learned in this chapter that any nursing or healthcare-related education you pursue will require many hours of clinical work, which includes hands-on practice with patients in real-world settings. The number of hours of clinical experience you need depends on the degree you choose to earn, as well as your own state's requirements. You might wonder how you can prepare for that experience and use fieldwork and/or internships to "test the waters," so to speak, so you can determine whether nursing really is for you.

This section helps point you to ways in which you can gain crucial experience in the nursing field before and during the time you're pursuing your education. This process can and should start in middle school or high school, especially during the summers. Experience is important for many reasons, including these:

- Shadowing others in the profession can help reveal what the job is really like and whether it's something you want to do day in and day out. This is a relatively risk-free way to explore different career paths. Ask any "seasoned" adult, and they will tell you that figuring out what you *don't* want to do is sometimes more important than figuring out what you *do* want to do.
- Internships and volunteer positions are a relatively quick way to gain work experience and develop job skills.
- Volunteering can help you learn the intricacies of the profession, such as what types of environments are best, what kind of care fits you better, and which areas are in more demand.
- Gaining experience during your high school years sets you apart from the many others who are applying to educational programs.
- Volunteering in the field means that you'll be meeting many others doing the job that you might someday want to do (think: career networking). You have the potential to develop mentor relationships, cultivate future job prospects, and get to know people who can recommend you for later positions. Studies show that about 85 percent of jobs are found through personal contacts.[13]

Experience can come in the form of volunteering at a local clinic or hospital, taking on an internship in the summer, finding a summer job that complements your interests, or even attending camps that foster your career aspirations (see www.teenlife.com to start). Consider these tidbits of advice to maximize your volunteer experience.[14] They will help you stand out in competitive fields.

- Get diverse experiences. For example, try to shadow at least two different types of nurses in different specialties and work settings.
- Try to gain forty hours of volunteer experience in each setting. This is typically considered enough to show that you understand what a full workweek looks like in that setting. You can commit as few as four to five hours per week over ten weeks or so.
- Find an aide/tech position. Working as a paid aide is by far the best experience you can get. This will prepare you nicely for your clinical experiences and tests as well.

Volunteering in a hospital setting is just one way to get real-world experience in caregiving.
© *Comstock/Stockbyte/Getty Images*

- Don't be afraid to ask questions. Just be considerate of the professionals' time and wait until they are not busy to pose your questions. Asking good questions shows that you have a real curiosity for the profession.
- Maintain and cultivate professional relationships. Write thank-you notes, send updates about your application progress, share where you decide to go to school, and check in occasionally. If you want to find a good mentor, you need to be a gracious and willing mentee.

If you're currently in high school and you're seriously thinking about becoming a nurse, reach out to a nurse in your own doctor's practice, or to a family friend who works as a nurse. Start by asking good questions and showing your curiosity. Ask to shadow this person if possible, remembering the guidelines about courtesy above. Don't expect to be paid for any of this effort. The benefit of volunteering is that it's much easier to get your foot in the door, but the drawback is that you typically are not paid. However, with time and hard work, your volunteer position may turn into a compensated role.

Look at these kinds of experiences as ways to learn about the profession, show people how capable you are, and make connections to others that could last your career. A volunteer position may even help you to get into the program of your choice, and it will definitely help you write your personal statement as to why you want to be a nurse.

Another way to find a position is to start with your high school guidance counselor or search the web for medical offices in your area. Don't be afraid to pick up the phone and call them. Be prepared to start by cleaning facilities, assisting staff with clerical work, and other such tasks. Being on-site, no matter what you're doing, will teach you more than you expect. With a great attitude and work ethic, you will likely be given more responsibility over time.

Once you are in your certificate or degree program, you will get many hours of hands-on experience as well.

> "Nursing school is very intense, just like the job. Hands-on skills are simulated in nursing school (on manikins, etc.), but until you are at the bedside and work with actual people, you can't be 100 percent prepared. Some stuff you just have to learn on the job."—Stacey Hummel, OB nurse department manager

Don't forget that your high school guidance counselor can be a great source of information and connections.

CALLED TO A NURSING CAREER

Sandra Gooden graduated from Purdue University with an associate's in nursing and returned to earn her BSN in 1990. She has worked almost her entire career in acute care environments—hospitals, critical care units, med-surg units, emergency rooms, recovery rooms, and step-down units. She's also been a manager and VP of nursing in Indiana and Illinois. She is currently a clinical nurse educator at a small county hospital.

How did you become interested in nursing?

No one in the family had gone to college. My parents were determined that my sister and I would go to college, though. I loved academics. I had my heart set on Purdue—it was close to home and the nursing program really appealed to me. I knew nurses older than me who had gone to Purdue and I understood that the college degree was important—not just a diploma. "You'll need those college credits someday," they told me. I was also interested in taking care of people.

When I was fourteen or fifteen, I got a job as a nurses' aide at the local community hospital. They took me under their wing and they really showed me the job. I fell in love with what the nurses were doing—they were so caring and I loved what they did with the patients. I saw those nurses doing wonderful things. I knew when I was fifteen or sixteen that I wanted to be a nurse—specifically, a Purdue nurse!

How would you describe your current position?

I am currently a clinical nurse educator at a small county hospital (about fifty beds—small). I mainly provide nursing orientations to newly hired RNs and unlicensed people. About 60 percent of my job is spent giving orientation classes, and 40 percent is involved with mandatory education and continuing education (such as learning new machines, updates on new procedures, etc.).

The continuation education stuff adds variety, which I like. No one reports to me and I report to someone outside the nursing department, so I have more freedom to focus on the bigger picture. You have to wear a lot of hats, see the big picture, and be objective, and I have a voice there. People listen to me and respect my opinion, which is nice. I don't have a lot of power to get things done, though.

The worst part is I don't have authority over who is hired or how changes happen, which can be frustrating.

Do you think your education prepared you for your job?

Yes, I do. Attending a nationally recognized nursing program like Purdue was extremely beneficial, even with the original ASN. I had a great science background. It's very rigorous and I had to work hard to get that degree. But once I got it, I knew I had something of value.

It prepared me to work at the bedside and it gave me a mindset about getting a BSN—I wish I would have gotten the BSN right away because I think I would have moved up more quickly. But life got in the way, as it does.

What's the best part of being a nurse?

Taking care of people is the most inspiring thing I have done. I see that I can make a difference in someone's life every day, even if it's a small thing. I can start IVs, draw blood, etc., so I can help other nurses do something tricky. I still enjoy doing things with my hands and helping patients, even after forty-three years. People respect you and they want you to help them. It's very gratifying.

What are some things in the nursing profession that are especially challenging right now?

The biggest frustration for nurses is that it's all about money and not about the people we are trying to serve. [Administrators] who don't understand the issues are the ones that control these important decisions. They don't understand what the job truly is, and they are in charge of the money for healthcare. They don't know what patients need, like a nurse and healthcare worker does.

What are some characteristics of a good nurse?

My mentors were the best—they were not at work for the money. They cared about the patients that they saw every day. They weren't afraid to be nice and caring and compassionate to people.

You don't get to be a nurse overnight—you work at it. Don't hold back. Let people know that you do care about them—all the other things will come.

Critical thinking skills make the best nurses adaptable. It's very important to have these skills. You must constantly juggle all these important options and decide which are important and which are not. You can watch and learn from the best.

What advice do you have for young people considering a career in nursing?

Nursing is a real career that is adaptable and flexible enough that you can continue to do it your whole life—a career that can change as you grow and change.

Nursing is a great career because of that. There is job security, especially when you are bedside. You can always land on your feet because there are so many ways you can go.

Look carefully at nursing schools and make sure you are picking a fully accredited school, *not* a for-profit school. I suggest getting a BSN from the get-go because you need those skills to do bedside adequately. Some ASN degrees focus on skills only and that is only part of the picture. Everyone needs a BSN to be fully qualified. Then, you can move on to get an MSN or DNP.

Being a nurse is a career, not a job! If you just want a job, don't be a nurse, because it's really hard.

How can a high schooler prepare for a career in nursing?

Take as many years of science as you can. It will prepare you better for college. You need a science background because the nursing curriculum is rigorous in terms of science.

Find out for yourself what nursing is like by volunteering in places where nurses work so you can see what they do day after day. It's not usually glamorous like some people think. It can be nitty-gritty. You have to understand the reality.

Work with a school nurse or volunteer at the local hospital—many positions are available to do that.

Any last thoughts?

We need more people who are not white and not female in nursing—we need more diversity in the nursing profession. And we need to entice others into the profession. Please don't mark us off your list until you fully investigate what nursing could offer you! We need more men and more people of color.

You can contribute to helping people. You can make a good living. You can be in positions of power now too. You are nobody's handmaiden. There is lots of room to move up in the career as well. It's a great profession!

Networking

Because it's so important, a last word about networking. It's important to develop mentor relationships, even at the early stages of your education. Remember that about 85 percent of jobs are found through personal contacts. If you know someone in the field, don't hesitate to reach out. Be patient and polite, but ask for help, perspective, and guidance.

If you don't know anyone who is a nurse, ask your school guidance counselor to help you make connections. Or pick up the phone yourself. Reaching out with a genuine interest in and a real curiosity about the field will go a long way. You don't need a job or an internship immediately—just a connection that could blossom into a mentoring relationship. Follow these important but simple rules for the best results when networking:

- Do your homework about a potential mentor, university, or employer before you make contact. Be sure to have a general understanding of what they do and why. But don't be a know-it-all. Be open and ready to ask good questions.
- Be considerate of professionals' time and resources. Think about what they can get from you in return for mentoring or helping you.
- Speak and write with proper English. Proofread all your letters, e-mails, and even texts. Think about how you will be perceived at all times.
- Always stay positive.

Summary

In this chapter, you learned even more about the different careers within the nursing umbrella—CNA, LPN, RN, and APRN—as well as the related degrees that each of those roles requires: certificate, associate's degree, bachelor's in nursing, master's in nursing, and the doctorate in nursing practice. You also learned about getting experience in these fields before you enter school as well as during the educational process. At this time, you should have a good idea of the educational requirements of each position. You hopefully have even contemplated which educational path fits your strengths, time constraints, and wallet.

Chapter 3 goes into more detail about pursuing the best educational path. It covers the process of researching schools and finding the best fit for your needs, as well as how to find the best value for your education. The chapter includes a discussion about financial aid and scholarships. At the end of chapter 3, you should have a much clearer view of the educational landscape and how and where you fit in.

3

Pursuing the Education Path

*W*hen it comes time to start looking at colleges, universities, or other postsecondary schools, many high schoolers tend to freeze up at the enormity of the job ahead of them. This chapter will help break down this process for you so it won't seem so daunting.

Yes, finding the right college or learning institution is important, and it's a big step toward achieving your career goals and dreams. Chapter 2 covered the various educational requirements of the nursing profession, which means you should now be ready to find the right institution of learning. This isn't always just a process of finding the very best school that you can afford and be accepted into, although that might end up being your path. It should also be about finding the right fit so that you can have the best possible experience during your post–high school years.

Here's the truth of it all: attending a postsecondary school isn't just about getting a degree. It's about learning how to be an adult, managing your life and your responsibilities, being exposed to new experiences, growing as a person, and otherwise becoming someone who contributes to society. College offers you an opportunity to actually become an interesting person with perspective on the world and empathy and consideration for people other than yourself.

An important component of how successful college will be for you is finding the right fit, the right school that brings out the best in you and challenges you at different levels. No pressure, right? Just as with finding the right profession, your ultimate goal should be to match your personal interests/goals/personality with the college's goals and perspective. For example, small liberal arts colleges have a much different feel and philosophy than big state schools. And rest assured that all this advice applies even when you're planning on attending community college or another postsecondary school.

This chapter dives into the nitty-gritty of finding the best schools, no matter what you want to do. In the healthcare field specifically, attending an accredited program is critical to future success.

Finding a School That Fits Your Personality

Before we get into the details of good schools, it will behoove you to take some time to consider what type of school will be best for you. If nothing else, answering the questions below may help you narrow your search and focus on a smaller sampling of choices. Write your answers to these questions down somewhere you can refer to them often, such as in the notes app on your phone.

- *Size*: Does the size of the school matter to you? College and university enrollments range from 500 or fewer students to upwards of 60,000.
- *Community location:* Would you prefer to be in a rural area, a small town, a suburban area, or a large city? How important is the location of the school in the larger world to you?
- *Distance from home:* How far away from home are you willing to go? Phrase this in terms of hours away or miles away.
- *Housing options:* What kind of housing would you prefer and can you afford? Dorms, off-campus apartments, and private homes are all common options.
- *Student body:* How would you like the student body to look? Think about coed versus all-male and all-female settings, as well as the percentage of minority students, how many students are part-time versus full-time, average age, and the percentage of commuter students.
- *Academic environment:* Consider which majors are offered and at which levels of degree. Research the student-faculty ratio. Are the classes taught often by actual professors or more often by teaching assistants? Find out how many internships the school typically provides to students. Are independent study or study abroad programs available in your area of interest?
- *Financial aid availability/cost:* Does the school provide ample opportunities for scholarships, grants, work-study programs, and the like? Does cost play a role in your options? (For most people, it does.)

- *Support services:* Investigate the strength of the academic and career placement counseling services of the school.
- *Social activities and athletics:* Does the school offer clubs that you are interested in? Which sports are offered? Are scholarships available?
- *Specialized programs:* Does the school offer honors programs or programs for veterans or students with disabilities or special needs?

Not all of these questions are going to be important to you, and that's fine. Be sure to also make note of aspects that don't matter so much to you, such as size or location. You might change your mind as you go to visit colleges, but it's important to consider your preferences up front.

Community colleges, as long as they are accredited, can be great places of learning for a fraction of the cost. © *martinedoucet/E+/Getty Images*

U.S. News & World Report puts it best when it says the college that fits you best is one that:

- Offers a degree that matches your interests and needs
- Provides a style of instruction that matches the way you like to learn
- Provides a level of academic rigor to match your aptitude and preparation
- Offers a community that feels like home to you
- Values you for what you do well[1]

According to the National Center for Educational Statistics (NCES), which is part of the US Department of Education, six years after entering college for an undergraduate degree, only 60 percent of students have graduated.[2]

Hopefully, this section has impressed upon you the importance of finding the right college fit. Take some time to paint a mental picture about the kind of university or school setting that will best complement your needs.

HOW IMPORTANT IS ACCREDITATION?

Accreditation is the process of ensuring that an academic program meets the common standards of quality set forth for that particular profession. Keep in mind that most companies will hire only people who received their degrees from programs that are accredited. This is especially true in the health-related fields such as nursing, which are more heavily regulated. When you research a school or program, make sure you can verify that the program of study is accredited through the proper accreditation body.

All of the following accrediting bodies keep databases of nursing programs. Check them out online for the most accurate and up-to-date lists of accredited schools.[3]

- **The Commission on Collegiate Nursing Education (CCNE)** (www.ccne accreditation.org) Accredits programs at the bachelor and graduate levels, as well as postgraduate APRN certificates and entry-to-practice nurse residency programs. CCNE is the autonomous accrediting arm of the American Association of Colleges of Nursing (AACN).

- **The Accreditation Commission for Education in Nursing (ACEN)** (www.acenursing.us/accreditedprograms/programSearch.htm) Accredits programs at the associate, diploma, bachelor, and graduate levels.
- **The Council on Accreditation of Nurse Anesthesia Educational Programs (COA)** (http://home.coa.us.com/accredited-programs/Pages/CRNA-School-Search.aspx) Accredits nurse anesthesia programs in the United States.
- **The Accreditation Commission for Midwifery Education (ACME), American College of Nurse-Midwives (ACNM)** (https://portal.midwife.org/education/accredited-programs) Accredits certificate, graduate nurse-midwifery, direct entry midwifery, and precertification nurse-midwifery education programs.

Researching Schools

If you're currently in high school and serious about pursuing a career in nursing, whether that's through a certificate, an associate's degree in nursing, a bachelor's degree in nursing , or more, start by finding four to five schools in a realistic location (for you) that offer the certificate/program/degree in question. Not every school near you or that you have an initial interest in will offer the program you want, of course, so narrow your choices accordingly. With that said, consider attending a university in your state of residency, if possible, which may save you lots of money. Private institutions don't typically discount resident student tuition costs.

Be sure you research the basic GPA and SAT or ACT requirements of each school.

Once you have found four to five accredited schools in realistic locations for you that offer the degree/certificate in question, spend some time on their websites studying the requirements for admissions. Most universities list the average stats for the last class accepted to the program. Important factors include whether or not you meet the school's requirements, your chances of getting in

For those of you applying to associate's degree programs or greater, most advisors recommend that you take both the ACT and the SAT during your junior year, in the spring at the latest. (The ACT is generally considered more weighted in science, so it may be more important for you as a prospective nursing student.) You can retake these tests and use your highest score, so don't leave yourself just one opportunity. You want your best score to be available to all the schools you're applying to by January of your senior year, especially if you are submitting any scholarship applications. Keep in mind that these are general timelines—be sure to check the exact deadlines and calendars of the schools to which you're applying!

(but shoot high!), tuition costs and availability of scholarships and grants, and the school's reputation and licensure/graduation rates.

The order of these characteristics will depend on your grades and test scores, your financial resources, and other personal factors. You of course want to find a program or school that has a good reputation for the science and health fields, but it's also important to consider your desired level of academic rigor and practical needs.

"Take your schooling seriously. Study the sciences, but don't limit yourself to them. Learn how to write and speak well."—Stacey Hummel, OB nurse department manager

What's It Going to Cost You?

So, the bottom line: what will your education end up costing you? Of course that depends on many factors, including the type and length of degree you pursue, where you attend (in state or not, private or public institution), how much in scholarships or financial aid you're able to obtain, your family or personal income, and many other factors. The National Center for Education Statistics (https://nces.ed.gov) tracks and summarizes financial data from colleges and universities all over the United States. A sample of recent data is shown in the following table on p. 58.

THE MOST PERSONAL OF PERSONAL STATEMENTS

The personal statement you include with your application to college is extremely important, especially when your GPA and SAT/ACT scores are on the border of what is typically accepted. Write something that is thoughtful and conveys your understanding of the nursing profession, as well as your desire to practice in this field. Why are you uniquely qualified? Why are you a good fit for this school? These essays should be highly personal (the "personal" in *personal statement*). Will the admissions professionals who read it, along with hundreds of others, come away with a snapshot of who you really are and what you are passionate about?

Look online for some examples of good personal statements, which will give you a feel for what works. Be sure to check your specific school for length guidelines, format requirements, and any other guidelines you are expected to follow.

Be sure to proofread your statement several times and ask a professional (perhaps someone in your school writing center or local library services) to proofread it as well.

Keep in mind that these are averages and reflect published prices, not net prices (see the following sidebar). If you read more specific data about a particular university or find averages in your particular area of interest, you should assume those numbers are closer to reality, as they are more specific. The College Board website (www.collegeboard.org) also has pertinent statistics.

Another way to look at it is that completion of an associate's degree (two years) costs about $25,000–$30,000. You can expect to pay about half that for a one-year nondegree certificate.

The actual, final price (or "net price") that you'll pay for a specific college is the published price (tuition and fees) minus any grants, scholarships, and education tax benefits you receive. This difference can be significant. In 2015–16, the average published price of annual in-state tuition and fees for public four-year colleges was about $9,410. But the average net price was only about $3,980.[5]

Table 3.1. Average Yearly Tuition, Fees, Room, and Board for Full-Time Undergraduates[4]

Year	Public 4-Year, In-State	Public 4-Year, Out-of-State	Private Nonprofit
2016–2017	$19,488	Not available	$41,465
2017–2018	$20,050	$25,657	$43,139

Source: The National Center for Education Statistics; nces.ed.gov

Generally speaking, there is about a 3 percent annual increase in tuition and associated costs to attend college. In other words, if you are expecting to attend college two years after this data was collected, you need to add approximately 6 percent to these numbers. This assumes there are no financial aid or scholarships of any kind.

WHAT IS A GAP YEAR?

Taking a year off between high school and college, often called a gap year, is normal, perfectly acceptable, and almost required in many countries around the world. It is becoming increasingly acceptable in the United States as well. Even Malia Obama, President Obama's daughter, did it. Because the cost of college has gone up dramatically, it literally pays for you to know going in what you want to study, and a gap year—well spent—can do lots to help you answer that question.

Some great ways to spend your gap year include joining the Peace Corps or AmeriCorps, enrolling in a mountaineering program or other gap year–styled program, backpacking across Europe or other countries on the cheap (be safe and bring a friend), finding a volunteer organization that furthers a cause you believe in or that complements your career aspirations, joining a Road Scholar program (www.roadscholar.org), teaching English in another country, or working to earn money for college!

Many students will find that they get much more out of college when they have a year to mature and to experience the real world. The American Gap Year Association reports from alumni surveys that students who take gap years show improved civic engagement, improved college graduation rates, and improved college GPAs.[6]

See the association's website at https://gapyearassociation.org for lots of advice and resources if you're considering this potentially life-altering experience.

Later in this chapter, you'll learn how to get your desired degree at an affordable price and how to get as much money for college as you can.

A WELL-ROUNDED NURSE WITH MANY JOB EXPERIENCES

Deb Newhouse.
Courtesy of Deb Newhouse

Deb Newhouse has been a nurse for forty-one years. Her first job was as an LPN, when she was twenty years old. She worked for many years as an LPN, mostly in a hospital setting. During that time, she also worked toward earning her associate's degree in nursing, through the Indiana University School of Nursing (Indianapolis). In 2008, she earned her BSN, also through the IU School of Nursing.

As an RN, she has worked in critical care cardiac surgery, as a patient care coordinator, in hospice case management, and in a medical ICU. She is currently working as an oncology nurse in a hospital setting.

How did you become interested in nursing?

I never thought about it as a teen, which was the early 1970s. But I was in a bad car accident when I was seventeen and was hospitalized for a few weeks. I had two very different nurses—one was burned out, not patient, without real concern or empathy. The other one "met me where I was." She knew I was hurt but also scared, and she was empathetic.

When I got out of the hospital, my mom pushed me to do something with my life. I saw that it could be worthwhile to be a nurse. Maybe I could provide hope and security to someone during a critical time in their life, like she [that nurse] did for me. LPN school was twelve months and it was relatively inexpensive. When I got to school, the lights went on and everything clicked.

How would you describe your current position?

I work at an outpatient medical oncology infusion center, which is a medical oncology clinic. The doctors and the nurse practitioners see patients and the infusion nurses give them medications (chemotherapy). It's fast-paced and different every day. You must be organized, have good personal skills with people, and be able to deal with ill and scared people.

The job includes physical assessments and treatments. It's fairly routine—you do labs too. People skills are key. Camaraderie with patients is the best part—the relationship with the patients is important. They appreciate that you can make a bad situation more pleasant.

Do you think your education prepared you for your job?

Nursing school gives you a sound base. You get out of it what you put in it. It requires lots of studying and dedication. You must be regimented and must put your all into it. I did that each time I went back to further my schooling. They don't spoon it to you—you have to be motivated to get what you need.

Continuing education is so important because healthcare is changing every day—new medications, better ways to assess people, new equipment, and so on. You have to keep up with it or it can be life and death. This includes free and pay-for education from your employer, in-services, and so on. Most of it is provided. Some states require credit hours of education each year to keep your license, such as Virginia.

What's the best part of being a nurse?

The patient contact. I missed that when I was a nurse educator. Interacting with patients and helping them and providing comfort is the best!

What are some current things in the nursing profession that are especially challenging?

The rate of change is really challenging. The new medications, tests, machines, treatment regimens, etc.—for example, the genetic testing for certain cancers. Keeping up with meds and the amount of information you can reach due to e-resources. Knowing which information you're reading is legitimate is important too.

The physical aspects of the bedside job are also difficult. More experienced nurses move to office settings and we continue to need bedside nurses. The baby boomer issue is important too.

What are some characteristics of a good nurse?

A good nurse is caring, honest, empathetic, has good moral ethics (chooses to do what's right with a patient), is patient with people, has an open mind, and tries to understand where the patients are coming from. That way, you can provide patients with the best information and help figure out what they need. I always try to remember that each patient is someone's loved one. I try to think how I would want my loved one to be treated.

What advice do you have for young people considering a career in nursing?

You should love science. You should also love biology and chemistry—this is paramount to the career. You have to understand the chemistry of the body. The nurses are the hands, eyes, and ears of the providers (doctor, nurse practitioner, physician assistant, etc.). The nurse reports the trends and issues with the patient to the provider. If you don't like science, you won't like being a nurse.

How can a high schooler prepare for a career in nursing?

Volunteer at or visit a retirement home and interact with the people there, even if it's just during their free time or activities. Get used to working with people who can't do everything for themselves. Get some experience.

After a year in school, you can get a job as a student tech, care tech, etc. Find a nurse mentor who can teach you and help you. You will be more comfortable when you get your first nursing job.

When you do graduate and get your first job, be prepared, as the first year is hard. But with experience, your level of knowledge will grow and grow. You learn by doing and with experience. You can't know everything on day one—the state boards really are the minimum knowledge you need.

Any last thoughts?

Do it if you love it—we need people who love it. It's a great career if you want to end up doing many different jobs with different skill sets, which will make you well-rounded.

Making the Most of School Visits

If it's at all practical and feasible, you should visit the schools you're considering. To get a real feel for any college or school, you need to walk around the campus and buildings, spend some time in the common areas where students hang out, and sit in on a few classes. You can also sign up for campus tours, which are typically given by current students. This is another good way to see the school and ask questions of someone in the know. Be sure to visit the specific school/building that covers your possible major. The website and brochures won't be able to convey that intangible feeling you'll get from a visit.

In addition to the questions listed earlier in this chapter, consider the queries below:

- What is the makeup of the current freshman class? Is the campus diverse?
- What is the meal plan like? What are the food options?
- Where do most of the students hang out between classes? (Be sure to visit this area.)
- How long does it take to walk from one end of the campus to the other?
- What types of transportation are available for students? Does campus security provide escorts to cars, dorms, etc., at night?

In order to be ready for your visit and make the most of it, consider these tips and words of advice. Before you go:

- Be sure to do some research. At the least, spend some time on the college website. Make sure your questions aren't addressed adequately there first.
- Make a list of questions.
- Arrange to meet with a professor in your area of interest or to visit the specific school or department.
- Be prepared to answer questions about yourself and why you are interested in this school.
- Dress in neat, clean, and casual clothes. Avoid overly wrinkled clothing or anything with stains.

Finally, be sure to send thank-you notes or e-mails after the visit is over. Remind the recipients of when you visited the campus and thank them for their time.

Financial Aid and Student Loans

Finding the money to attend college, whether it is a two- or four-year institution, an online program, or a vocational career college, can seem overwhelming. But you can do it if you have a plan before you actually start applying to college. If you get into your top-choice school, don't let the sticker cost turn you away. Financial aid can come from many different sources and it's available to cover all different kinds of costs you'll encounter during your years of study, including tuition, fees, books, housing, and food.

The good news is that colleges and universities often offer incentives or tuition discount aid to encourage students to attend. The market is often more competitive in favor of the student, and colleges and universities are responding by offering more generous aid packages to a wider range of students than they used to. Here are some basic tips and pointers about the financial aid process:

- Apply for financial aid during your senior year. You must fill out the Free Application for Federal Student Aid (FAFSA) form, which can be filed starting October 1 of your senior year until June of the year you graduate.[7] Because the amount of available aid is limited, it's best to apply as soon as you possibly can. See https://studentaid.ed.gov/sa/fafsa to get started.
- Compare and contrast the offers you get from different schools. There is room to negotiate with most institutions. See if your top-choice school will match or beat the best aid package you received.
- To be eligible to keep and maintain your financial aid package, you must meet certain grade/GPA requirements. Be sure you are very clear on these academic expectations and keep up with them.
- You must reapply for federal aid every year.

It's important to understand the different forms of financial aid that are available to you. That way, you'll know how to apply for different kinds and get the best financial aid package that fits your needs and strengths. The two main categories that financial aid falls under are gift aid, which doesn't have to be repaid, and self-help aid, which includes loans that must be repaid and work-study funds that are earned. The next sections cover the various types of financial aid that fit in these categories.

Paying for college can take a creative mix of grants, scholarships, and loans, but you can find your way with some help. © *Casper1774Studio/iStock/Getty Images Plus*

Watch out for scholarship scams! You should never be asked to pay to submit the FAFSA form ("free" is in its name) or to find appropriate aid and scholarships. These are free services. Promises that you'll get aid or that you have to "act now or miss out" are both warning signs of a less than reputable organization.

Also, be careful with your personal information to avoid identity theft. Simple things like closing and exiting your browser after visiting websites where you entered personal information (like studentaid.ed.gov) goes a long way. Don't share your student aid ID number with anyone, either.

GRANTS

Grants typically are awarded to students who have financial need, but can also be used in the areas of athletics, academics, demographics, veteran support, and special talents. They do not have to be paid back. Grants can come from federal agencies, state agencies, specific universities, and private organizations. Most federal and state grants are based on financial need.

Examples of grants are the Pell Grant, the SMART Grant, and the Army Nurse Corps Grant. The Health Resources and Services Administration (HRSA) sponsors several valuable grants specifically designed for nursing students. See http://bhpr.hrsa.gov/nursing.

Some federal grants are for nursing professionals willing to work in states or communities (including Indian reservations) that have been traditionally underserved with healthcare.

SCHOLARSHIPS

Scholarships are merit-based aid that does not have to be paid back. They are typically awarded based on academic excellence or some other special talent, such a music or art. Scholarships also can be athletic-based, minority-based, aid for women, and so forth. These are typically not awarded by federal or state governments, but instead come from the specific school you applied to as well as private and nonprofit organizations.

Be sure to reach out directly to the financial aid officers of the schools you want to attend. These people are great contacts who can lead you to many more sources of scholarships and financial aid. Visit the GoCollege website at www.gocollege.com/financial-aid/scholarships/types for lots more information about how scholarships in general work.

LOANS

Many types of loans are available, especially to students to pay for their postsecondary education. However, the important thing to remember here is that loans must be paid back, with interest. (This is the extra cost of borrowing the money and is usually a percentage of the amount you borrow.) Be sure you understand the interest rate you will be charged. Is it fixed or will it change over time? Are payments on the loan and interest deferred until you graduate (meaning you don't have to begin paying it off until after you graduate)? Is the loan subsidized (meaning the federal government pays the interest until you graduate)? These are all points you need to be clear about before you sign on the dotted line.

There are many types of loans offered to students, including need-based loans, non-need-based loans, state loans, and private loans. Two very reputable federal loans are the Perkins Loan and the Direct Stafford Loan. For more information about student loans, visit the College Board's "BigFuture" website at https://bigfuture.collegeboard.org/pay-for-college/loans/types-of-college-loans.

FEDERAL WORK-STUDY

The US federal work-study program provides part-time jobs for undergraduate and graduate students with financial need so they can earn money to pay for educational expenses. The focus is on community service work and work related to a student's course of study. Not all schools participate in this program, so be sure to check with the school financial aid office if this is something you are counting on. Funds are limited, so the sooner you apply, the more likely you will get the job you desire and be able to benefit from the program. Visit the US Department of Education's Federal Student Aid website at https://studentaid.ed.gov/sa/types/work-study for more information about this opportunity.

FROM ER NURSE TO NURSE EDUCATOR

Kara Schalk.
Courtesy of Kara Schalk

Kara Schalk graduated from Purdue University with a bachelor's degree in institutional management. While working as the human resources director for a long-term healthcare facility, she became interesting in nursing. She subsequently earned her ASN in 1993 and worked as an LPN nurse for eighteen years. She then got her BSN in 2012 and her MSN/RN in education in 2016.

Schalk has worked as a nurse in a variety of settings—in emergency rooms, in pediatric outpatient, in a trauma center, and in a geriatric hospital. Most of it was outpatient care. In 2016, she became a network-based educator to four ER departments, all part of a large healthcare network.

How did you become interested in nursing?

Working in HR in a nursing home at my first profession, I felt like I was doing a disservice to my employer by not knowing what the employees (the nurses) did. I interviewed and hired nurses at that time, and I wanted to further my education so I could serve the position better. I found myself very interested in learning what nurses did and looked into returning to school. At the same time, a staff development nurse that I really liked was leaving and I knew I wanted her job. I wanted to be able to educate and to be a nurse, to marry both aspects. I liked the idea of becoming a nurse so I could be a nurse developer and educator.

What are your main job duties?

My current role is as a network-based educator for four ER departments of a large health network in Indianapolis, Indiana. I facilitate, guide, and support the ER educators. I provide standardized education across the ERs, based on evidence-based practice. The network is huge. My job is to pull it all together and provide comprehensive, standardized education without gaps.

As an example, all ER nurses must have advanced cardiac life support (ACLS) training. I am an ACLS instructor. I keep up on the standards and curriculum and make sure that ER staff all get all the same, updated curriculum. I also bring in SMEs (subject matter experts), who educate staff on specific new procedures or new pieces of equipment. I educate the ER guys, which they then disseminate to their staff.

Do you think your education prepared you for your job?

It absolutely did. My master's program was through University of Indianapolis, which was fantastic. You have to be an expert in at least two fields to be a nurse educator. I had twenty-five years of nursing experience in the outpatient setting. I worked in the ER for eighteen years, so I was an expert in that field. I have also been teaching for five to six years. I owe my mentors over the years for teaching me as well.

What's the best part of being a nurse?

I enjoy being in a service profession. It's an honor. It's very valuable and meaningful to me to help other people.

What is the most surprising thing about being a nurse?

I have literally had a hand in saving people's lives. In the moment, you do what you need to do as a nurse. Later, after the chaos in the ER is over, you realize you helped save them. That's astonishing sometimes.

What are some things that are especially challenging?

Nursing today is different than it was twenty-five years ago. Nurses used to be more autonomous and independent thinkers. They aren't as much now.

I am not a fan of the 100 percent online degrees or the accelerated programs. You don't get the human/patient touch, which really is the essence of nursing. Nursing is a practice-based discipline.

Nursing is much more task-oriented now, which takes away the independence of it, including the people skills and the subtle decision-making skills that nurses learn on the job while dealing with people.

What are some characteristics of a good nurse?

You must be an independent thinker and be able to multitask critically. You also need to be a strong time manager. You should be intelligent, articulate, and self-motivated. Compassion and empathy are important too.

People who can't deal with gray areas don't do as well in nursing. Healthcare involves many life circumstances, so there are often no real absolutes. You have to be okay, for example, if someone wants to die.

To be successful at nursing, you have to love it, because it's physically and mentally demanding. Don't just do it because you heard the hours are good.

What are some of the current challenges facing nursing and the people in it?

The aging nursing population and baby boomers are both challenges. There are more older patients and more people entering the system. At the same time, there aren't enough careers and not enough places to put people. We need more nurses, which is why these pop up, accelerated programs were started. Many nurses in these accelerated programs are not prepared when they get out of school—the academic-to-practice gap is much larger than it was years ago. In the past, new nurses did not work in critical care until they had at least one year of experience in outpatient or on a standard floor under their belt. Now, because of the nursing shortage, they go right to critical care. Burnout is high.

What advice do you have for young people considering a career in nursing?
Consider *why* you want to be a nurse. If you are a service-directed person who wants to give back, that's great—nursing needs you desperately! But don't serve until you are completely empty. Work/life balance is important. You have to take time to yourself and regenerate and "fill your cup up." It should be a calling, but be ready to take care of yourself too. If you're just in it for the money, don't bother.

How can a high schooler prepare for a career in nursing?
Volunteer however you can—in a hospital, in an extended care facility. Any service-oriented job will help you learn the ropes. The service industry teaches you how to deal with others. You have to deal with all kinds of different people.

Any last thoughts?
Ultimately, if you think you want to do something, do it! Don't have regrets. Even if it means switching careers, which is what I did. Sometimes those people make the best nurses.

Find your passion. Take care of yourself.

Making High School Count

If you are approaching or still in high school, there are many things you can do now to help the postsecondary educational process go more smoothly. Consider these tips for your remaining years:

- Work on listening well and speaking and communicating clearly. Work on writing clearly and effectively.

- Learn how to learn. This means keeping an open mind, asking questions, asking for help when you need it, taking good notes, and doing your homework.
- Plan a daily homework schedule and keep up with it. Have a consistent, quiet place to study.
- Talk about your career interests with friends, family, and counselors. They may have connections to people in your community whom you can shadow or who will mentor you.
- Try new interests and activities, especially during your first two years of high school.
- Be involved in extracurricular activities that truly interest you and say something about who you are and who you want to be.

Kids are under so much pressure these days to "do it all," but you should think about working smarter rather than harder. If you are involved in things you enjoy, your educational load won't seem like such a burden. Be sure to take

Volunteering is a great way to get résumé-worthy experience and find out if you really love the job.
© Milkos/iStock/Getty Images Plus

time for self-care, such as sleep, unscheduled downtime, and activities that you find fun and energizing. See chapter 4 for more ways to relieve and avoid stress.

> "Taking care of people is the most inspiring thing I have done. I see that I can make a difference in someone's life every day, even if it's a small thing."
> —Sandra Gooden, clinical nurse educator

Summary

This chapter talked about all the aspects of college and postsecondary schooling that you'll want to consider as you move forward. Remember that finding the right fit is especially important, as it increases the chances that you'll stay in school and finish your degree or program—and have an amazing experience while you're there. The nursing careers covered in this book have varying educational requirements, which means that finding the right school is specific to your career aspirations.

In this chapter, you learned how to get the best education for the best deal. You also learned a little about scholarships and financial aid, how the SAT and ACT work, and how to write a unique personal statement that eloquently expresses your passions.

Use this chapter as a jumping-off point to dig deeper into your particular area of interest, but don't forget these important points:

- Take the SAT and ACT early in your junior year so you have time to take them again. Most schools automatically accept the highest scores.
- Make sure that the school you plan to attend has an accredited program in your field of study. This is particularly important in the nursing field. Some professions follow national accreditation policies, while others adhere to state-mandated policies and therefore differ across state lines. Do your research and understand the differences.
- Don't underestimate how important school visits are, especially in the pursuit of finding the right academic fit. Come prepared to ask questions not addressed on the school website or in the literature.

- Your personal statement is a very important piece of your application that can set you apart from other applicants. Take the time and energy needed to make it unique and compelling.
- Don't assume you can't afford a school based on the sticker price. Many schools offer great scholarships and aid to qualified students. It doesn't hurt to apply. This advice especially applies to minorities, veterans, and students with disabilities.
- Don't lose sight of the fact that it's important to pursue a career that you enjoy, are good at, and are passionate about! You'll be a happier person if you do so.

At this point, your career goals and aspirations should be jelling. At the very least, you should have a plan for finding out more information. And don't forget about networking, which was covered in detail in chapter 2. Remember to do research about the school or degree program before you reach out and especially before you visit. Faculty and staff find students who ask challenging questions much more impressive than those who ask questions that can be answered by spending ten minutes on the school's website.

Chapter 4 goes into detail about the next steps, writing a résumé and cover letter, interviewing well, sending follow-up communications, and more. This information is not just for college grads; you can use it to secure internships, volunteer positions, summer jobs, and other opportunities. In fact, the sooner you can hone these communication skills, the better off you'll be in the professional world.

Writing Your Résumé and Interviewing

*N*o matter which path you decide to take—whether you enter the work-force immediately after high school, go to college first and then find yourself looking for a job, or maybe do something in between—having a well-written résumé and impeccable interviewing skills will help you reach your ultimate goals. This chapter provides some helpful tips and advice about how to build the best résumé and cover letter, how to interview well with all your prospective employers, and how to communicate effectively and professionally at all times. The advice isn't just for people entering the workforce full-time. It can help you score that internship or summer job or help you give a great college interview to impress the admissions office.

This chapter also has some tips for dealing successfully with stress, which is an inevitable by-product of a busy life.

CARING FOR OTHERS IS IN HIS BLOOD

Marc Gavilanez.
Courtesy of Marc Gavilanez

Marc Gavilanez received his ASN from Lutheran College of Health Professions in 1993, returning to school to earn a bachelor's degree in biology. His first job was on a general med-surg floor in a small community hospital, where he worked for three years. He then worked at an outpatient surgery center for five years. He and his wife then spent ten years in Vietnam as missionaries doing community health work. In 2010, they returned to the United States and he worked again as a nurse in the outpatient surgery setting. In 2017, Marc moved to an orthopedic outpatient surgery center. He has been a nurse for twenty-six years.

How did you become interested in nursing?

My dad was an OB/GYN and my mom was a nurse. My sister is a physician assistant. So it's in my blood! It's what we talked about around the dinner table. We also took family medical mission trips when I was a child. It's always been a part of my life. I was originally thinking about physical therapy school, but I realized in college that wasn't what I wanted to do. I had worked as a nurse's aide during the summers and that was really interesting to me.

The surgery component was interesting—I had some experience there and I liked being a part of a surgery team and seeing that process in action.

What are your main job duties as a surgery center nurse?

I am an OR (operating room) circulator. A circulator nurse works right in the OR—we meet patients preop and talk to them and their families. We gather the patient's history, get the room ready, get the supplies set up, and so on.

We then get the patient from preop and prep the surgery room. The doctor comes in with their team. We keep records and manage the supplies during the procedure. We ready any meds that might be needed. After the surgery, we take the patient to the recovery room nurse. We report to the nurse how the surgery went, wound instructions, and other postop instructions. My day might include as many as five to six cases.

My side jobs throughout the day include pulling cases and supplies for the next day, stocking supplies and rooms, doing morning checks on equipment, meeting with committees, and so on. The OR nurse basically manages the surgery center and keeps it running smoothly.

Do you think your education prepared you for your job?

I earned my ASN to add to my bachelor's in biology and I am certified as an RN. I am also currently getting my bachelor's degree in nursing. The health system I moved to a few years ago requires its nurses to have a bachelor's in nursing within five years of being hired. That's becoming the norm.

Yes, I do think it prepares you well. To sit for the RN licensing exam, you have to be prepared. The education gives you a nice, broad perspective. The clinicals helped me see what area of nursing I might be interested in.

When you have a real job, you will get on-the-job training that's specialized to what you are doing. Although my education did prepare me as much as possible, some of it you just have to learn on the job.

What's the best part of being a nurse?

Helping people! Every day, you come away feeling like you have helped someone. It could be a traumatic life event and you are a part of making it better. It's a social job and you get to meet lots of patients and families and you work on a team. I am a social person, so I like that. The coworkers and the teams really add to the quality of the job.

The hours are very nice as well. At the surgery center where I work, there are no on-call times, no weekend hours, and no holiday hours. I work four days a week, ten-hour shifts. I like that.

What is the most surprising thing about your current job?

My job will pay for me to get my bachelor's, which is a great benefit. Our health system is strong in the area and doing well financially. They pass that along as periodic raises to us, which is nice.

What are some things that are especially challenging?

You have to be a lifelong learner. Things change often and you have to keep up. In the busy times, certifications come up and they can add to the load.

For example, OR nurses need to be continuously certified in areas like basic life support (similar to CPR), advanced cardiac life support (ACLS), and pediatric advanced life support (PALS), which must be renewed every year or two years. That means that every six months, you are probably renewing one of these. You can also be certified as an OR nurse, and there is a two- to five-year timeframe to recertify for that (it's not required, however).

What are some characteristics of a good nurse?

You have to want to help people, be caring, and be empathetic. The best nurses are good listeners. You must not mind the sight of blood. Nurses need to be flexible as well. If you don't like working on a team and you don't want to be a lifelong learner, it's probably not the profession for you.

What are some of the current challenges facing nursing and the people in it?

Computerized charting is expensive initially (the equipment and the training), and it can be difficult to adjust to. It can be efficient, but it can seem to patients that we are more interested in getting info into a computer than connecting to them. You sometimes lose that personal touch. Obviously, it has benefits, like centralized storage of information, but we are losing that personal touch when we are so tied down to technology.

I have also noticed that rising healthcare costs can negatively affect the patient's view of their healthcare treatment.

What advice do you have for young people considering a career in nursing? How can a high schooler prepare for a career in nursing?

Interview people who work in the field you're interested in and ask questions. Ask them about the good, the bad, and the ugly.

Also, job shadow! Follow a nurse around at the job—more than one day if possible. If you can be talked out of it by what you see or hear, nursing may not be for you. If you see all the good, bad, and ugly and are still interested, that's a good sign. Summer jobs in healthcare would be smart too.

For new nursing grads, I suggest that you look for a job early on that gives you broad experience (the "renting before buying" approach); then you can get more specific/specialized as you know what you really like. Med-surg floors provide good broad experience. Or try out the telemetry (monitoring) floors to start out if you are interested in cardiac treatment, med-surg, ICU, and so on.

Any last thoughts?

In general, I want to encourage other guys to enter the nursing field. There is still a very low percentage of men in nursing. This has been a good career for me as a man in terms of being able to support my family. You can support your family, male or female. It's also a job that travels—you can easily switch your licensure and move from state to state and find jobs all over. You can also step out for a few years and step back in. It's a very healthy profession and lots of people are retiring, so we need more nurses!

Writing Your Résumé

If you're a teen writing a résumé for your first job, you likely don't have a lot of work experience under your belt yet. Because of this limited work experience, you need to include classes and coursework that are related to the job you're seeking, as well as any school activities and volunteer experience you have. While you are writing your résumé, you might discover some talents and recall some activities that you forgot about, but that are still important to add. Think about volunteer work, side jobs you've held (babysitting, dog walking, etc.), and the like. A good approach at this point is to build a functional résumé, which focuses on your abilities rather than work experience.

PARTS OF A RÉSUMÉ

As mentioned, the functional résumé is the best approach when you don't have a lot of pertinent work experience, as it is written to highlight your abilities rather than your experience. (The other, perhaps more common, type of résumé is called the chronological résumé; it lists a person's accomplishments in chronological order, most recent jobs first.) This section breaks down and discusses the functional résumé in greater detail.

Here are the essential parts of your résumé, listed in the order they should appear:

- *Heading*: This should include your name, address, and contact information, including phone, e-mail, and website if you have one. This information is typically centered at the top of the page.
- *Objective:* This is one sentence that tells the employer what kind of position you are seeking. It should be modified to be specific to each potential employer.
- *Education:* Always list your most recent school or program first. Include date of completion (or expected date of graduation), degree or certificate earned, and the institution's name and address. Include workshops, seminars, and related classes here as well.
- *Skills:* Skills include computer literacy, leadership skills, organizational skills, and time-management skills. Be as specific in this area as possible.
- *Activities:* Activities can be related to skills. Perhaps an activity listed

here helped you develop a skill listed above. This section can be combined with the Skills section, but it's often helpful to break these apart if you have enough substantive things to say in both areas. Examples include sports teams, leadership roles, community service work, clubs and organizations, and so on.

- *Experience:* If you don't have any actual work experience that's relevant, you might consider skipping this section. However, you can list summer, part-time, and volunteer jobs you've held.
- *Interests:* This section is optional, but it's a chance to include special talents and interests. Keep it short, factual, and specific.
- *References:* It's best to say that references are available on request. If you do list actual contacts, include no more than three and make sure you inform your contacts that they might be contacted.

The first three parts above are pretty much standard, but the others can be creatively combined or developed to maximize your abilities and experience. These are not set-in-stone sections that every résumé must have. As an example, consider the mock functional résumé that follows.

If you're still not seeing the big picture here, it's helpful to look at student and part-time résumé examples online to see how others have approached this process. Search for "functional résumé examples" to get a look at some examples.

RÉSUMÉ-WRITING TIPS

Regardless of your situation and why you're writing a résumé, there are some basic tips and techniques you should use:

- Keep it simple. This includes using simple language and a standard font and format. Using one of the résumé templates provided by your word processing software can be a great way to start.
- Keep it short—to one page if possible.
- Highlight your academic achievements, such as a high GPA (above 3.5) and academic awards. If you have taken classes related to the job you're interviewing for, list those briefly as well.
- Emphasize your extracurricular activities, internships, and the like. These could include clubs, sports, dog walking, babysitting, or volunteer work. Use these activities to show your skills and abilities.

Ryan William Corcoran

620 River Road
Portland, OR, 97035
Phone: 503-503-5030 E-Mail: rwc2004@student.com

Objective

Seeking an entry-level position to further my passion and desire to work in the healthcare industry as a nurse

Education

High School Diploma, June 2020
Henry James High School, Portland, OR
GPA: 3.94. Top 2% of class

Skills

Computer literacy on PC and Mac; MS Word, Excel, PowerPoint, desktop publishing, web software
Trained in first aid and CPR
Four years of Spanish

Activities

Captain of the Spanish Club, 2019
Outstanding Community Service Award, 2018
Volunteer tutor of Spanish to ESL students, 2018-2019

Experience

2018 co-op volunteer participant, Standport Long-Term Care Facility, Portland OR
June 2017-June 2019, Part-time volunteer, Primrose Hospital, Portland, OR
May 2016-June 2017, Crew Team Member, Big Burger Stop 'N Eat, Portland, OR

References

Available upon request

A functional-style résumé is a good template to use when you don't have a lot of work experience.

- Use action verbs, such as *led, created, taught, ran*, and *developed*.
- Be specific and give examples.
- Always be honest.
- Include leadership roles and experience.
- Edit and proofread at least twice and have someone else do the same. Ask a professional (such as someone in your school writing center or local library services) to proofread it for you also. Don't forget to run spell check.
- Include a cover letter (discussed next).

THE COVER LETTER

Every résumé you send out should include a cover letter. This can be the most important part of your job search because it's often the first thing that potential employers read. By including a cover letter, you're showing employers that you took the time to learn about their organization and address them personally. This goes a long way toward proving that you're interested in the position.

Be sure to call the company or verify on the website the name and title of the person to whom you should address the letter. This letter should be brief. Introduce yourself and begin with a statement that will grab the person's attention. Keep in mind that employers potentially receive hundreds of résumés and cover letters for every open position. You want yours to stand out. Important information to supply in the cover letter, in order from the top, includes:

- Your name, address, phone number, and e-mail address
- The current date
- The recipient's name, title, company name, and company address
- A salutation

Then you begin the letter portion of the cover letter, which should mention how you heard about the position, something extra about you that will interest the potential employer, practical skills you can bring to the position, and past experience related to the job. You should apply the facts outlined in your résumé to the job to which you're applying. Each cover letter should be personalized for the position and company to which you're applying. Don't use "To whom it may concern." Instead, take the time to find out to whom you should actually address the letter. Finally, end with a complimentary closing, such as "Sincerely, Henry Smith," and be sure to add your signature. Search the internet for "sample cover letters for internships" or "sample cover letters for high schoolers" to see some good examples.

If you are e-mailing your cover letter instead of printing it out, you'll need to pay particular attention to the subject line of your e-mail. Be sure that it is specific to the position you are applying for. In all cases, it's important to follow the employer's instructions about how to submit your cover letter and résumé. Generally speaking, sending PDF documents rather than editable documents is a better idea. Everyone can read a PDF, whereas word processing documents may require specific software to access. Most word processing programs have an option under the Save command that allows you to save your work as a PDF.

> "Continuing education is so important because healthcare is changing every day—new medications, better ways to assess people, new equipment, and so on. You have to keep up with it or it can be life and death."—Deb Newhouse, oncology nurse

EFFECTIVELY HANDLING STRESS

As you're forging ahead with your life plans—whether it's college, a full-time job, or even a gap year—you might find that these decisions feel very important and heavy and that the resulting stress is difficult to deal with. That's completely normal. Try these simple stress-relieving techniques:

- Take deep breaths in and out. Try this for thirty seconds. You'll be amazed at how it can help.
- Close your eyes and clear your mind.
- Go scream at the passing subway car. Or lock yourself in a closet and scream. Or scream into a pillow. For some people, screaming can really help.
- Keep the issue in perspective. Any decision you make now can be changed if it doesn't work out.

Want to avoid stress altogether? It is surprisingly simple. Of course, simple doesn't always mean easy, but the following ideas are basic and make sense based on what we know about the human body:

- Get enough sleep.
- Eat healthy.
- Get exercise.
- Go outside.
- Schedule downtime.
- Connect with friends and family.

The bottom line is that you need to take time for self-care. There will always be stress in your life, but how you deal with it makes all the difference. This becomes increasingly important as you enter college or the workforce and maybe have a family. Developing good, consistent habits related to self-care now will serve you all your life.

"To be successful at nursing, you have to love it, because it's physically and mentally demanding. Don't just do it because you heard the hours are good."
—Kara Schalk, network-based nurse educator

Developing Your Interview Skills

The best way to avoid nerves and keep calm when you're interviewing is to be prepared. It's okay to feel scared, but keep it in perspective. It's likely that you'll receive many more rejections than acceptances in your professional life, as we all do. However, you need only one "yes" to start out. Think of the interviewing process as a learning experience. With the right attitude, you will learn from each experience and get better with each subsequent interview. That should be your overarching goal. Consider these tips and tricks[1] when interviewing, whether it's for a job, internship, college admission, or something else entirely:

- Practice interviewing with a friend or relative. Practicing will help calm your nerves and make you feel more prepared. Ask for specific feedback from your friends. Do you need to speak louder? Are you making enough eye contact? Are you actively listening when the other person is speaking?
- Learn as much as you can about the company, school, or organization. Also be sure to understand the position for which you're applying. This will show the interviewer that you are motivated and interested in the organization.
- Speak up during the interview. Convey to the interviewer important points about yourself. Don't be afraid to ask questions. Try to remember the interviewers' names and call them by name.
- Arrive early and dress professionally and appropriately. (You can read more about proper dress in a following section.)
- Take some time to prepare answers to commonly asked questions. Be ready to describe your career or educational goals to the interviewer.

Common questions you may be asked during a job interview include these:

- Tell me about yourself.
- What are your greatest strengths?
- What are your weaknesses?
- Tell me something about yourself that's not on your résumé.
- What are your career goals?
- How do you handle failure? Are you willing to fail?
- How do you handle stress and pressure?
- What are you passionate about?
- Why do you want to work for us?

Common questions you may be asked during a college admissions interview include these:

- Tell me about yourself.
- Why are you interested in going to college?
- Why do you want to major in this subject?
- What are your academic strengths?
- What are your academic weaknesses? How have you addressed them?
- What will you contribute to this college/school/university?

- Where do you see yourself in ten years?
- How do you handle failure? Are you willing to fail?
- How do you handle stress and pressure?
- Whom do you most admire?
- What is your favorite book?
- What do you do for fun?
- Why are you interested in this college/school/university?

Jot down notes about your answers to these questions, but don't try to memorize the answers. You don't want to come off as too rehearsed during the interview. Remember to be as specific and detailed as possible when answering these questions. Your goal is to set yourself apart in some way from the other people who will interview. Always accentuate the positive, even when you're asked about something you did not like, or about failure or stress. Most important, though, be yourself.

Active listening is the process of fully concentrating on what is being said, understanding it, and providing nonverbal cues and responses to the person talking.[2] It's the opposite of being distracted and thinking about something else when someone is talking. Active listening takes practice. You might find that your mind wanders and you need to bring it back to your conversational partner (and this could happen multiple times during one conversation). Practice this technique in regular conversations with friends and relatives. In addition to helping you give a better interview, it can cut down on nerves and make you more popular with friends and family, as everyone wants to feel that they are really being heard. For more on active listening, check out the MindTools website at www.mindtools.com/CommSkll/ActiveListening.htm.

You should also be ready to ask questions of your interviewer, ones that aren't answered on the web or in the company or school literature. Asking questions shows that you are interested and have done your homework. Avoid asking questions about salary/scholarships or special benefits at this stage, and don't mention anything negative that you've heard about the company or school. Keep the questions positive and related to the position to which you're applying. Some example questions to potential employers include:

- What is a typical career path for a person in this position?
- How would you describe the ideal candidate for this position?
- How is the department organized?
- What kind of responsibilities come with this job? (Don't ask this if it has already been addressed in the job description or discussion.)
- What can I do as a follow-up?
- When do you expect to reach a decision?

See the section in chapter 3 entitled "Making the Most of School Visits" for some good example questions to ask the college admissions office. The important thing is to write your own questions related to answers you really want to know. This will show genuine interest. Be sure your question isn't answered on the website, in the job description, or in the literature.

DRESSING APPROPRIATELY

It's important to determine in advance what will be appropriate in the setting of the interview. What is appropriate in a corporate setting might be different from what you'd expect at a small liberal arts college or in a large hospital setting. Most college admissions offices suggest "business casual" dress, but for a job interview, you may want to step it up from there. Again, it's important to do your homework and come prepared. In addition to reading any available guidelines, it never hurts to take an advance look around the site to see what other people are wearing to work or to interviews. Regardless of the setting, make sure your clothes are not wrinkled, untidy, or stained. Avoid flashy clothing of any kind.

FOLLOW-UP COMMUNICATION

Be sure to follow up, whether via e-mail or regular mail, with a thank-you note to the interviewer. This is true whether you're interviewing for a job or internship or interviewing with a college. A handwritten thank-you note, posted in the actual mail, is best. In addition to being considerate, it will trigger the interviewer's memory about you and show that you have genuine interest in

Even something like "business casual" can be interpreted in many ways, so do some research to find out what exactly is expected of you. © *asiseeit/E+/Getty Images*

the position, company, or school. Be sure to follow a standard business letter format and highlight the key points of your interview and experience at the company/university. And be prompt with your thank-you! Put it in the mail the day after your interview (or send that e-mail the same day).

Knowing What Employers Expect

Regardless of the job, profession, or field you end up working in, there are universal characteristics that all employers (and schools, for that matter) look for in potential employees. At this early stage in your professional life, you have an opportunity to recognize which of these foundational characteristics are your strengths (and therefore highlight them in your résumé and interviews) and which are weaknesses (and therefore continue to work on them and build them up). Consider these universal characteristics that all employers look for:

- Positive attitude
- Dependability

- Desire to continue to learn
- Initiative
- Effective communication
- Cooperation
- Organization

This is not an exhaustive list; other desired characteristics might include sensitivity, honesty, good judgment, loyalty, responsibility, and punctuality. Specifically in healthcare/nursing, you can add flexibility, empathy, being detail-oriented, having a caring nature, and being able to multitask to that list. Consider these important characteristics when you answer the common questions that employers ask. It pays to work these traits into your answers, of course being honest and realistic about your personal qualities.

Beware the social media trap! Prospective employers and colleges will check your social media profile, so make sure there is nothing too personal, explicit, or inappropriate on your sites. When you communicate to the world via social media, don't use profanity but do be sure to use proper grammar. Think about the version of yourself you are portraying online. Is it favorable or at least neutral to potential employers? They will look, rest assured.

Personal contacts can make the difference! Don't be afraid to contact people you know. Personal connections can be a great way to find jobs and internship opportunities. Your high school teachers, your coaches and mentors, and your friends' parents are all examples of people who may know about jobs or internships that would suit you. Start asking several months before you hope to start a job or an internship, because it will take some time to do research and arrange interviews. You can also use social media in your search. LinkedIn (www.linkedin.com), for example, includes lots of searchable information on local companies. Follow and interact with people on social media to get their attention. Just remember to act professionally and communicate with proper grammar, just as you would in person.

Summary

Well, you made it to the end of this book! Hopefully, you have learned enough about the nursing field to start your journey or to continue on your path. If you feel like nursing is right for you, that's great news. If you've figured out that this isn't the right field for you, that's good information too. For many of us, figuring out what we *don't* want to do and what we *don't* like is an important step in finding the right career.

With a little hard work and perseverance, you'll be on your way to career success!
© djiledesign/iStock/Getty Images Plus

There is a lot of good news about the nursing field in this book! It's a very smart career choice for anyone with a passion to help people. It's fulfilling, lucrative, flexible, not monotonous, and easily customizable. Job demand is high and will continue to grow in the foreseeable future.

Whether you decide to attend a four-year university, get an associate's degree, earn a certificate, or take a gap year, having a plan and an idea about your future can help guide your decisions. After reading this book, you should be well on your way to having a plan for your future. Good luck to you as you move ahead!

Glossary

accreditation: The act of officially recognizing an organizational body, person, or educational facility as having a particular status or being qualified to perform a particular activity. For example, schools and colleges are accredited. *See also* certification.

ACT: One of the standardized college entrance tests that anyone wanting to enter undergraduate studies in the United States should take. It measures knowledge and skills in mathematics, English, reading, and science reasoning as they apply to college readiness. There are four multiple-choice sections and an optional writing test. The highest score possible on the ACT is 36. *See also* SAT.

active listening: The process of fully concentrating on what is being said, understanding it, and providing nonverbal cues and responses to the person talking. It's the opposite of being distracted and thinking about something else when someone is talking to you.

advanced practice registered nurses (APRNs): Nurses who have at least a master's degree in nursing (MSN), although many employers require them to have a doctorate of nursing practice (DNP). APRNs serve specialized roles in the healthcare field—as nurse practitioners, certified nurse-midwives, clinical nurse specialists, and certified registered nurse anesthetists.

anesthesia: Medicine given so that surgery and other medical process can be performed on patients without them feeling any pain, and in many situations, without patients being awake or conscious during the procedure. There are many types of anesthesia.

anatomy: The area of science concerned with the bodily structure and organization of humans, animals, and other living things.

associate's degree: A degree awarded by a community or junior college that typically requires two years of study.

baby boomers: The American generation born after WWII, from about 1945 until about 1964. During this time, there was a "boom" (large increase) in the number of births in the United States. This matters to professionals in healthcare, and specifically nursing, because baby boomers continue to age and disproportionally need the care and services that nurses provide.

bachelor's degree: An undergraduate degree awarded by a college or university that typically requires a four-year course of study when pursued full-time (this can vary by the degree earned and by the university awarding the degree). The BSN is a bachelor's of science in nursing.

cardiovascular system: The system of the human body comprising the heart and blood, including veins and arteries. Related diseases include stroke, heart attack, and high blood pressure.

certification: The action or process of confirming that an individual has acquired certain skills or knowledge, usually provided by some third-party review, assessment, or educational body. Individuals, not organizations, are certified. *See also* accreditation.

certified nursing assistants (CNAs): Caregivers who help patients with their daily activities, such as bathing, dressing, and eating. CNA training involves learning the basic nursing principles and working hands-on in supervised clinical settings. You can get CNA training at vocational colleges, community colleges, and technical schools.

certified nurse-midwives (CNMs): APRNs who specialize in delivering babies and providing gynecological and low-risk obstetrical care. This specialty requires at least an MSN (master of science in nursing degree). *See also* advanced practice registered nurses (APRNs).

certified registered nurse anesthetists (CRNAs): APRNs who work with surgeons, anesthesiologists, dentists, podiatrists, and other professionals to ensure safe use of anesthesia. This specialty requires at least an MSN (master of science in nursing degree). *See also* advanced practice registered nurses (APRNs).

clinical nurse specialists (CNSs): APRNs who handle a range of physical and mental health problems. They have the skills and expertise to identify where the gaps are in healthcare. They often help design and implement interventions and assess and evaluate those to improve overall healthcare. This specialty requires at least an MSN (master of science in nursing degree). *See also* advanced practice registered nurses (APRNs).

diagnosis: When a healthcare professional determines the nature of an illness or problem after examining a patient.

doctorate: The highest degree awarded by colleges and universities. It qualifies the holder to teach at the university level and requires (usually published) research in the field. After earning a bachelor's degree, a student may need an additional three to six years earn the doctorate. Anyone with a doctorate can be addressed as "doctor," not just medical doctors. The doctorate of nursing practice (DNP) is the nursing version.

gap year: A year between high school and college (or sometimes between college and postgraduate studies) during which the student is not in school but is instead involved in volunteer programs (such as the Peace Corps), in travel experiences, or in work and teaching experiences.

grants: Money to pay for postsecondary education that is typically awarded to students who have financial needs, but can also be used in the areas of athletics, academics, demographics, veteran support, and special talents. Grants do not have to be paid back.

license: An official document, card, or certificate that gives you permission to have, use, or do something, such as practice as a registered nurse. Typically, one gets certified and then applies for a license.

licensed practical nurses (LPNs): Nurses who support the healthcare team and work under the supervision of an RN, APRN, or MD. LPNs must complete one year of academic training through a diploma or certificate program, although many pursue an associate's degree (ADN—usually two years). Some of their duties include checking patient vital signs and performing basic nursing functions such as changing bandages and wound dressings.

master's degree: A postgraduate degree awarded by colleges and universities that requires at least one additional year of study after a bachelor's degree. The degree holder shows mastery of a specific field. The MSN is a master of science in nursing degree.

National Council Licensure Examination (NCLEX): A nationwide examination that nursing graduates must take in order to be licensed (and work) as nurses in the United States and Canada. There are two versions: the NCLEX-RN (for registered nurses) and the NCLEX-PN (for practical nurses). The examinations are developed and owned by the National Council of State Boards of Nursing, Inc. (NCSBN).

nurse practitioners (NPs): APRNs who prescribe medication, diagnose and treat minor illnesses and injuries, order and interpret diagnostic and laboratory tests, and create treatment plans. This specialty requires at least an MSN (master of science in nursing degree). *See also* advanced practice registered nurses (APRNs).

pathology: The science that identifies and manages diseases.

personal statement: A written description of your accomplishments, outlook, interest, goals, and personality that's an important part of your college application. The personal statement should set you apart from other applicants. The required length depends on the institution, but personal statements generally range from one to two pages, or 500 to 1,000 words.

physician assistants (PAs): Medical personnel who are licensed to diagnose and treat illness and disease and to prescribe medication to patients. They work in physician offices, hospitals, and clinics in collaboration with a licensed physician. Their education, which is more in line with the medical model than the nursing model, requires a bachelor's of science, a twenty-five-month accredited physician assistant program, and a one-year clinical rotation.

postsecondary degree: An educational degree above and beyond a high school education. This is a general description that includes trade certificates and certifications, associate's degrees, bachelor's degrees, master's degrees, and beyond.

registered nurses (RNs): Nurses who provide and coordinate patient care, educate patients and the public about various health conditions, and provide advice and emotional support to patients and their family members. RNs usually pursue a bachelor of science in nursing (BSN), but some get an associates degree in nursing (ADN). Some employers—especially hospitals—require a bachelor's degree. Registered nurses must also be licensed, by passing the National Council Licensure Examination (NCLEX-RN).

rehabilitation: The process of returning someone back to a healthier state or a more functional life after an illness or accident.

SAT: One of the standardized tests in the United States that anyone applying to undergraduate studies should take. It measures verbal and mathematical reasoning abilities as they relate to predicting successful performance in college. It is intended to complement a student's GPA and school record in assessing readiness for college. The highest score possible on the SAT is 1600. *See also* ACT.

scholarships: Merit-based aid used to pay for postsecondary education that does not have to be paid back. Scholarships are typically awarded based on academic excellence or some other special talent, such as music or art.

Notes

Introduction

1. Bureau of Labor Statistics Occupational Outlook Handbook, "Registered Nurses," https://www.bls.gov/ooh/healthcare/registered-nurses.htm.

2. Stephen P. Juraschek, Xiaoming Zhang, Vinoth K. Ranganathan, and Vernon Lin, "United States Registered Nurse Workforce Report Card and Shortage Forecast," *American Journal of Medical Quality* 27, no. 3 (2012): 241–49, https://digitalcommons.unl.edu/cgi/viewcontent.cgi?article=1148&context=publichealthresources.

3. Paul Barr, "Baby Boomers Will Transform Health Care as They Age," Hospitals and Health Networks, January 14, 2014, https://www.hhnmag.com/articles/5298-Boomers-Will-Transform-Health-Care-as-They-Age.

4. Alia Paavola, "The Importance of Preventive Care Strategies in a Changing Healthcare Environment," Becker's Hospital Review, September 19, 2017, https://www.beckershospitalreview.com/population-health/the-importance-of-preventive-care-strategies-in-a-changing-healthcare-environment.html.

5. Susan W. Salmond and Mercedes Echevarria, "Healthcare Transformation and Changing Roles for Nursing," *Orthopedic Nursing* 36, no. 1 (2017): 12–25, https://www.ncbi.nlm.nih.gov/pmc/articles/PMC5266427/.

6. American Association of Colleges of Nursing, "Fact Sheet: Nursing Shortage," updated April 2019, https://www.aacnnursing.org/Portals/42/News/Factsheets/Nursing-Shortage-Factsheet.pdf.

Chapter 1

1. Global Pre-Meds, "Certified Nursing Assistant: Qualifications, Job Description, and Career Prospects," December 6, 2013, https://www.gapmedics.com/blog/2013/12/06/certified-nursing-assistant-qualifications-job-description-career-prospects/.

2. Bureau of Labor Statistics Occupational Outlook Handbook, "Nursing Assistants and Orderlies," https://www.bls.gov/ooh/healthcare/nursing-assistants.htm.

3. Nurse Journal, "LPN vs. RN Roles and Responsibilities," https://nursejournal .org/practical-nursing/lpn-vs-rn-roles/.

4. American Nurses Association, "What Is Nursing?" https://www.nursingworld .org/practice-policy/workforce/what-is-nursing/.

5. Bureau of Labor Statistics Occupational Outlook Handbook, "Licensed Practical and Licensed Vocational Nurses," https://www.bls.gov/ooh/healthcare /licensed-practical-and-licensed-vocational-nurses.htm.

6. Nurse Journal, "LPN vs. RN Roles and Responsibilities."

7. Bureau of Labor Statistics Occupational Outlook Handbook, "How to Become a Registered Nurse," https://www.bls.gov/ooh/healthcare/registered-nurses. htm#tab-4.

8. American Association of Colleges of Nursing, "Fact Sheet: The Impact of Education on Nursing Practice," updated April 2019, https://www.aacnnursing.org /Portals/42/News/Factsheets/Education-Impact-Fact-Sheet.pdf.

9. Institute of Medicine, National Academies, *The Future of Nursing: Leading Change, Advancing Health*, October 5, 2010, http://nationalacademies.org/hmd /reports/2010/the-future-of-nursing-leading-change-advancing-health.aspx.

10. All Nursing Schools, "Everything Nurses Need to Know about the NCLEX Licensing Exam," https://www.allnursingschools.com/how-to-become-a-nurse/nclex -exam/.

11. American Nurses Association, "What Is Nursing?"

12. Bureau of Labor Statistics Occupational Outlook Handbook, "Registered Nurses," https://www.bls.gov/ooh/healthcare/registered-nurses.htm.

13. American Nurses Association, "What Is Nursing?"

14. National Association of Clinical Nurse Specialists, "What Is a CNS?" https:// nacns.org/about-us/what-is-a-cns/.

15. American Nurses Association, "What Is Nursing?"

16. Bureau of Labor Statistics Occupational Outlook Handbook, "Nurse Anesthetists, Nurse Midwives, and Nurse Practitioners," https://www.bls.gov/ooh/health care/nurse-anesthetists-nurse-midwives-and-nurse-practitioners.htm.

17. Bureau of Labor Statistics Occupational Outlook Handbook, "Nurse Anesthetists, Nurse Midwives, and Nurse Practitioners: Work Environment," https:// www.bls.gov/ooh/healthcare/nurse-anesthetists-nurse-midwives-and-nurse-practi tioners.htm#tab-3.

18. ExploreHealthCareers.org, "Physician Assistant," https://explorehealthcareers .org/career/medicine/physician-assistant/.

19. American Academy of PAs, "Become a PA," https://www.aapa.org/career-central/become-a-pa/.

20. ExploreHealthCareers.org, "Physician Assistant."

21. Bureau of Labor Statistics Occupational Outlook Handbook, "Physician Assistants," https://www.bls.gov/ooh/healthcare/physician-assistants.htm.

22. Bureau of Labor Statistics Occupational Outlook Handbook, "Physician Assistants: Job Outlook," https://www.bls.gov/ooh/healthcare/physician-assistants.htm#tab-6.

23. Swati Kapoor, "Ten Qualities That Make a Good Nurse," *Minority Nurse* (blog), July 5, 2016, https://minoritynurse.com/10-qualities-that-make-a-great-nurse/.

Chapter 2

1. NursingLicensure.org, "Certified Nurse Assistant Requirements in California," https://www.nursinglicensure.org/cna/california-nursing-assistant.html.

2. Learn How to Become, "How to Become a Licensed Practical Nurse: LPN/LVN Programs and Careers," https://www.learnhowtobecome.org/nurse/licensed-practical-nurse/.

3. Nursing.org, "ADN Guide: Nursing Associates Degree," https://www.nursing.org/degrees/associate/.

4. Ibid.

5. Institute of Medicine, National Academies, *The Future of Nursing: Focus on Education*, October 2010, http://www.nationalacademies.org/hmd/Reports/2010/The-Future-of-Nursing-Leading-Change-Advancing-Health/Report-Brief-Education.aspx.

6. Linda H. Aiken, Sean P. Clarke, Robyn B. Cheung, Douglas M. Sloane, and Jeffrey H. Silber, "Educational Levels of Hospital Nurses and Surgical Patient Mortality," *Journal of the American Medical Association* 290, no. 12 (2003): 1617–23, https://jamanetwork.com/journals/jama/fullarticle/197345.

7. Nursing.org, "Bachelor's Degree in Nursing (BSN)," https://www.nursing.org/degrees/bachelors/.

8. Wikipedia, "National Council Licensure Examination," https://en.wikipedia.org/wiki/National_Council_Licensure_Examination.

9. Nursing.org, "Master's Degree in Nursing (MSN)," https://www.nursing.org/degrees/masters/.

10. Ibid.

11. American Association of Colleges of Nursing, "DNP Education," https://www.aacnnursing.org/Nursing-Education-Programs/DNP-Education.

12. Nursing.org, "Doctor of Nursing Practice Degree (DNP)," https://www.nursing.org/degrees/dnp/.

13. Lou Adler, "New Survey Reveals 85% of All Jobs Are Filled via Networking," LinkedIn.com, February 29, 2016, https://www.linkedin.com/pulse/new-survey-reveals-85-all-jobs-filled-via-networking-lou-adler/.

14. Mathew Hilton, "Leverage Your Volunteering Experience When Applying to Physical Therapy School," CovalentCareers.com, May 11, 2016, https://covalent careers.com/resources/volunteer-experience-physical-therapy-school/.

Chapter 3

1. Peter Van Buskirk, "Finding a Good College Fit," *U.S. News & World Report*, June 13, 2011, https://www.usnews.com/education/blogs/the-college-admissions-insider/2011/06/13/finding-a-good-college-fit.

2. National Center for Education Statistics, "Fast Facts: Graduation Rates," https://nces.ed.gov/fastfacts/display.asp?id=40.

3. NursingCAS, "What's the Deal with Accreditation?" March 12, 2018, https://www.nursingcas.org/whats-the-deal-with-accreditation/.

4. National Center for Education Statistics, "Tuition Costs of Colleges and Universities," https://nces.ed.gov/programs/digest/d18/tables/dt18_330.20.asp.

5. College Board/BigFuture, "Understanding College Costs," https://bigfuture.collegeboard.org/pay-for-college/college-costs/understanding-college-costs.

6. Gap Year Association, "Research Statement," https://gapyearassociation.org/research.php.

7. Federal Student Aid, US Department of Education, "FAFSA Changes for 2017–2018," https://studentaid.ed.gov/sa/about/announcements/fafsa-changes

Chapter 4

1. Justin Ross Muchnick, *Teens' Guide to College & Career Planning*, 12th ed. (Lawrenceville, NJ: Peterson's, 2015), 179–80.

2. MindTools, "Active Listening: Hear What People Are Really Saying," https://www.mindtools.com/CommSkll/ActiveListening.htm.

Resources

*A*re you looking for more information about the nursing field or even about a branch within healthcare in general? Do you want to know more about the college application process or need some help finding the right educational fit for you? Do you want a quick way to search for a good college or school? Try these resources as a starting point on your journey toward finding a great career!

Books

Cunningham, Kevin. *Nurse.* 21st Century Skills Library: Cool Steam Careers. Ann Arbor, MI: Cherry Lake, 2015.

Field, Shelly. *Career Opportunities in Health Care*, 3rd ed. New York: Checkmark Books, 2007.

Fiske, Edward. *Fiske Guide to Colleges.* Naperville, IL: Sourcebooks, 2018.

Gresham, Barbara B. *Today's Health Professions: Working Together to Provide Quality Care.* Philadelphia: F.A. Davis, 2016.

Muchnick, Justin Ross. *Teens' Guide to College & Career Planning*, 12th ed. Lawrenceville, NJ: Peterson's, 2015.

Princeton Review. *The Best 382 Colleges, 2018 Edition: Everything You Need to Make the Right College Choice.* New York: Princeton Review, 2018.

Websites

Accrediting Bureau of Health Education Schools
www.abhes.org
This accrediting agency is recognized by the US Department of Education and by the Council for Higher Education Accreditation. The website includes a list of accredited institutions and programs, a calendar of upcoming events, a special tab for students, a section on recent publications, and much more.

Accreditation Commission for Education in Nursing
www.acenursing.us
The ACEN accredits nursing programs at the associate, diploma, baccalaureate, and graduate levels. Visit the website for a full list of accredited programs in your area.

American Association of Colleges of Nursing
www.aacnnursing.org
The AACN calls itself "the national voice for academic nursing." Its stated purpose is to work to establish quality standards for nursing education. That includes assisting schools in implementing the standards, influencing the nursing profession to improve healthcare, and promoting public support for professional nursing education, research, and practice.

American Gap Year Association
www.gapyearassociation.org
The American Gap Year Association's mission is "making transformative gap years an accessible option for all high school graduates." A gap year is a year taken between high school and college to travel, teach, work, volunteer, generally mature, and otherwise experience the world. The website has lots of advice and resources for anyone considering taking a gap year.

American Nurses Association
www.nursingworld.org
The goal of the ANA is to "improve patient care through supporting individuals and organizations to advance the nursing profession. From advocating in the halls of Congress, to setting the bar for credentialing worldwide, the ANA Enterprise exists to give every nurse the best chance of success." The website contains information about nursing certifications, credentialing programs, and nursing practice and policy standards.

The Balance
www.thebalance.com
This site is all about managing money and finances, but it also has a large section called Careers, which provides advice for writing résumés and cover letters,

interviewing, and more. Search "teens" on the site and you will find teen-specific advice and tips.

The College Board
www.collegeboard.org
The College Board tracks and summarizes financial data from colleges and universities all over the United States. This well-organized site can be your one-stop shop for all things college research. It contains lots of advice and information about taking and doing well on the SAT and ACT, many articles on college planning, a robust college search feature, a scholarship search feature, and a major and career search area. You can type your career of interest (for example, registered nurse) into the search box and get back an overview page that describes the career, gives advice on how to prepare for it, suggests where to get experience, identifies characteristics you should have to excel in this career, lists helpful classes to take while in high school, and provides lots of links to more information.

CollegeGrad Career Profiles
www.collegegrad.com/careers
Although this site is primarily geared toward college graduates, the career profiles area has a list of links to nearly every career you could ever think of. A single click takes you to a very detailed, helpful section that describes the job in detail, explains the educational requirements, includes links to good colleges that offer training in this career and to actual open jobs and internships, describes the licensing requirements (if any), lists salaries, and much more.

Commission on Accreditation of Allied Health Education Programs
www.caahep.org
CAAHEP is one of the largest programmatic accreditors in the health sciences field. The website enables you to easily search through a large collection of accredited programs. It also includes a specific section just for students and a news and events section.

Explore Health Careers
www.explorehealthcareers.org
As the title suggests, this site enables you to explore careers in the health fields.

You can seek answers to questions such as whether a career in health is for you, find the right fit and focus your search within the many fields, actually find the job or internship you're looking for, learn more about paying for college, and more.

Kahn Academy
www.khanacademy.org
The Kahn Academy website is an impressive collection of articles, courses, and videos about many educational topics in math, science, and the humanities. You can search any topic or subject (by subject matter and grade) and read lessons, take courses, and watch videos to learn all about it. The site includes test prep information for the SAT, ACT, AP, GMAT, and other standardized tests. There is also a college admissions section with lots of good articles and information, provided in the approachable Kahn style.

Live Career
www.livecareer.com
This site has an impressive number of resources directed toward teens for writing résumés and cover letters and preparing for interviews.

Mapping Your Future
www.mappingyourfuture.org
This site helps young people figure out what they want to do and maps out how to reach career goals. It includes helpful tips on résumé writing, job hunting, job interviewing, and more.

Monster
www.monster.com
This is perhaps the most well-known and certainly one of the largest employment websites in the United States. You fill in a couple of search boxes and away you go. You can sort by job title, of course, as well as by company name, location, salary range, experience range, and much more. The site also includes information about career fairs, advice on résumés and interviews, and more.

National Council of State Boards of Nursing
www.ncsbn.org
The NCSBN "empowers and supports nursing regulators in their mandate to protect the public." One of the council's primary functions is to develop and oversee the National Council Licensure Examination (NCLEX), an exam for nurse licensure in the United States and Canada. There are two versions of this exam: the NCLEX-RN (registered nursing) and the NCLEX-PN (practical nursing). All nurses must sit for and pass one of the two exams, depending on their role, in order to practice nursing in the United States and Canada.

NursingLicensure.org
www.nursinglicensure.org
This site calls itself "a more efficient way to find nursing licensing requirements in your state" and includes a clickable map of all fifty states, where you'll find information about all of the nursing license requirements, applications, and exams required by your state of residence.

Occupational Outlook Handbook
www.bls.gov/ooh
The US Bureau of Labor Statistics produces this website, which offers lots of relevant and updated information about various careers, including median salaries, how to work in the industry, the job market outlook, typical work environments, and what workers do on the job. See www.bls.gov/emp/ for a full list of employment projections.

Peterson's
www.petersons.com
In addition to lots of information about preparing for the ACT and SAT and easily searchable information about scholarships nationwide, the Peterson's site includes a comprehensive search feature for universities and schools based on location, major, name, and more.

Sigma

www.sigmanursing.org

Sigma is the second-largest nursing organization in the world, with approximately 135,000 active members. The site includes an active job board, online member forums, a calendar of upcoming conferences and other nursing events, a resources tabbed reference for students, and a marketplace of Sigma products, including books and more.

Study.com

www.study.com

Similar to Kahn Academy, this site lets you search any topic or subject and read lessons, take courses, and watch videos to learn all about it. It includes a good collection of information about nursing and the basic science and medicine knowledge needed to excel in nursing school.

TeenLife

www.teenlife.com

This site calls itself "the leading source for college preparation" and includes lots of information about summer programs, gap year programs, community service, and more. It argues that spending time "in the world," outside of the classroom, can help students develop important life skills. This site contains many links to volunteer and summer programs.

U.S. News & World Report *College Rankings*

www.usnews.com/best-colleges

U.S. News & World Report provides almost fifty different types of numerical rankings and lists of colleges throughout the United States to help students with their college search. You can search colleges by best reviewed, best value for the money, best liberal arts schools, best schools for B students, and more.

About the Author

Kezia Endsley is an editor and author from Indianapolis, Indiana. In addition to editing technical publications and writing books for teens, she enjoys running and triathlons, traveling, reading, and spending time with her family and many pets.

Editorial Board